The Failing Logic of Money

The Transition to a World
Free from Suffering

The Failing
Logic of Money

The Transition to a World
Free from Suffering

Duane Mullin

BOOKS

Winchester, UK
Washington, USA

First published by O-Books, 2011
O-Books is an imprint of John Hunt Publishing Ltd., Laurel House, Station Approach,
Alresford, Hants, SO24 9JH, UK
office1@o-books.net
www.o-books.com

For distributor details and how to order please visit the 'Ordering' section on our website.

Text copyright: Duane Mullin 2010

ISBN: 978 1 84694 259 4

A CIP catalogue record for this book is available from the British Library.

Design: Stuart Davies

Printed in the UK by CPI Antony Rowe
Printed in the USA by Offset Paperback Mfrs, Inc

We operate a distinctive and ethical publishing philosophy in all
areas of our business, from our global network of authors to
production and worldwide distribution.

CONTENTS

Foreword   ix
Acknowledgements   xii
Introduction   1

Book One. Where We Are   7

1. The Current Financial System   8
2. Four Thousand Years of Progress but No Real Change   20
3. The Impact of Money on Society   28
4. Why Money Economies Cause Unnecessary Hunger
    & Starvation   45
5. Our Current Political Options and How Money
    Controls All   50
6. The Impact of Money on Individuals   59
7. The Role of Technology in a Monetary Society   66
8. Conclusion to Book One   71

Book Two. An Alternative.   73

9.   A Different Way of Doing Things – Earth Economics   74
10. What Would Earth Economics Mean to People?   79
11. What Would a Earth Economics Mean to Society?   85
12. Conclusion to Book Two   105

Book Three. How To Get There.   107

13. Can Society Change?   108
14. What We Must Change in Ourselves?   112
15. Questions to Ask Yourself   117
16. The Action We Must Take   121
17. Conclusion to Book Three   138

Postscript   141

The New Citizen's Agreement with Society   142

Appendix:
Proving the Link Between Crime & Poverty   148

References & Notes   151

Further Reading   159

Foreword

Once upon a time in a land very close to each of us lived a man and the time was..... let's say it was roughly about now. In this wonderful rich land were some sacred cows. These cows had clearly once been glorious strong creatures but were now past their best and in much need of medical attention, if not a humane end to their suffering. Atop these faded creatures that trembled under the weight sat an emperor. These emperors sat large and haughty, proud and impressive. From their privileged place atop the sacred cows, the emperors issued edicts and commands (some of which were very cruel and heartless) that kept the population of people very, very busy and very, very tired and very, very sad. But as large and impressive as these emperors were, they were totally and entirely naked, not a stitch of clothing. It wasn't a pretty sight. Well, the day came when the man (who was busy following orders from the emperors just like everyone else) looked up from his labours and turned to his neighbour. The man wiped the sweat from his brow and said, "Is it me or do the sacred cows need a vet and maybe to be retired?" His neighbour said, "I'm too busy following orders to look. Get back to work". And the man did.

After a little while the man looked up from his labours again and turned to his neighbour, he wiped the sweat from his brow and said "Is it me but aren't the emperors, for whom we all work so hard, aren't they naked and very ugly, selfish and cruel?" His neighbour quickly looked up and saw how ridiculous the emperors were and how weak and pitiful the sacred cows were and he saw just how fragile it all was. Because it would all tumble with the slightest breeze.

The neighbour scurried quickly back to work and worked even harder to please the emperors and the sickly beasts they rode on. The man said "Well? Did you see it?"

The neighbour turned to the man with tears streaming down his face, "we all know it, we just don't talk about it.......but what else can we do. Will we not all perish without them?"

And the man turned to his neighbour and said "I have a plan for a better life".

This book will introduce new ideas and challenge some of the sacred cows upon which our society and civilisation has been built. These sacred cows are now sickly, putrid and polluting the nations and the people they once served. As an academic, it was clear that the social sciences of economics, politics and their subordinate disciplines such as marketing, accounting etc have been intended to address the issues of being human. Until now I always considered that our financial system was imperfect but the best available way of addressing our common human needs.

This is no longer true.

Our forebears over the years have found ingenious ways of keeping our present financial system going by developing increasingly sophisticated ways of "propping up" the beasts and the naked emperors, rather than deal with the underlying and causative issue, the fact they are no longer relevant or useful. This book deals head on with the cause and constructively posits an alternative that would logically work. Maybe it is time the beasts were retired rather than forced to struggle on, maybe it is time we all looked at our emperors and saw just how naked, ugly and cruel they are, maybe it is time we retired them too.

Our current economic woes are likely to emerge and re-emerge with increasing frequency and more devastating effect because a successful economy depends upon exquisitely balanced opposing forces and drives. A money economy has never yet provided every human with a home, full employment, enough to eat and dignity. We have never achieved the impossible perfect equilibrium needed to solve human problems in our entire history, because it is just that, impossible under a money system.

There will always be those that cannot find food to eat and those emperors that simply do not care. Over the years humans have been in a constant state of war, crime and hatred. We have devoted human ingenuity to developing ingenious ways of killing and hurting each other, we have hunted entire species of animal until there is not one single living soul left and yet we do not learn. We do not put our creativity into addressing human needs. We are squandering our gift.

But there is another way. It works. The only problem is the emperors atop their putrid sacred cows may not like it and may howl and thrash about. But they are so fragile, despite the pride and impressive display.

I commend this book as a heartfelt attempt from a man to alert his neighbour that there is an alternative to submitting to the cruel emperors who only have power because we tolerate them. My only concern is that fear of change will cause the neighbour to return to his labours; struggling, suffering and dying, while the tears stream from his eyes.

John Pope BA(Hons) in Economics
MA in Politics and Government
Diploma in Marketing
PGCE

Acknowledgements

To start the debate towards a better world for us and our children.

This is to express my appreciation for those that have contributed to the completion of this book, you know who you are, but a special thank you to Shane Gadd for helping me gather the internal resources and concentration needed to turn a moment of realisation into a work worth sharing.

To my long standing friend Christopher Pick N.D. for always having a useful opinion and expressing it vigorously.

For ease of reading, instead of he/she or variations of this (which I find clumsy), I will be using the traditional 'he' to refer to both genders.

Failure is the opportunity to begin again more intelligently
Henry Ford

Once a republic is corrupted, there is no possibility of remedying any of the growing evils but by removing the corruption.
Thomas Jefferson

Introduction

What is the point of an economy?

The objective of any economy (whether it's the hunter/gatherer way of our ancestors or our current capitalist and communist systems), is to address the challenges of having a frail human body. All economies use or convert the earth's resources into items needed by people, this could be a cave-dweller converting a stone or stick into a hunting tool or a corporation converting unrefined oil into a product currently needed for transport. The only difference between the multi-national corporation and the cave-dweller is the sophistication of the goods and services created. The other challenge all economies face is how to ensure the goods and services created end up with the people that need or want them.

The imperative to convert the earth's raw resources into goods people want/need, then distribute the result has been a problem as old as humankind itself. Early humans solved this challenge using free resource sharing among small groups or family but quickly moving to barter and labour exchange to distribute the results of their work as their community grew in numbers. More recently people developed trade and currency to address the same issues the cave-dweller had to contend with. But with any system, it should be periodically reviewed and its effectiveness evaluated and where necessary a better way of achieving the same aims presented.

This book is effectively a simple review of how well we have done in achieving the objectives of any economy, which is to ensure the physical needs and material well being of people. This book also intends to propose and support a hypothesis that using money to achieve the aims of an economy is bound to create unsatisfactory outcomes. So let's look at where we are today.

This was written between 2008 and 2010 in a prosperous country against a backdrop of economic turmoil (failing banking institutions, falling house prices, failing businesses, reposessions, foreclosures and the world's economies sliding into recession), whilst banking executives pay themselves enviable cash bonuses and walk away from the mess they helped engender. There are rising food and energy prices, growing unemployment and genuine fear and insecurity being experienced by normal working families who are increasingly losing the opportunity to earn a living whilst a few people have abundance.[1] This gap is expected to have widened in the Bush years and the pattern is not dissimilar in all modern economies. In Britain with a government that claims to be socially responsible and seeks to reduce the gap between rich and poor, the National Equality Panel has found that the differential in Britain is at its worst since WW2 despite [Telegraph Newspaper 27 Jan 2010] a decade of efforts to stop it.

As a result, in the prosperous countries, government is preparing for an increase in crime and violence as people become desperate to maintain a standard of living at the expense of those around them.[2] Our quality of life is falling because we find ourselves less able to pay for what we want or we are afraid that our employment status may change for the worse, rather than the goods and services not being available.

It should be noted that in a recession, money does not disappear, it just moves to different people i.e. bailiffs, debt administrators, banks and basic/subsistence goods and services suppliers. Money for general purchases seems to have disappeared but in reality most of it was never there in the first place, and what was there simply moves into fewer hands.

This is happening against a backdrop of war conducted in oil rich states under the guise of providing human rights to its citizens whilst the civil rights of those in countries without interesting resources are more easily ignored.

The less prosperous countries are experiencing food riots (recently in Egypt, Haiti, Ivory Coast and Cameroon and there have been food price demonstrations in Italy, Indonesia and many other places). As people try to avoid the spectre of hunger or starvation, the sheer desperation in these countries leads to the debasement of human nature – whilst corrupt leaders are more concerned about providing cash security for themselves and friends than acting in the interests of people they should serve, (another form of poverty crime). Ironically, the food shortages were not caused by any inability of the planet to provide us with what we need; the cause of the food shortages was the incentives and inducements offered to the agriculture industry to grow bio-fuel crops instead of food as well as the emerging economies picking up western eating habits. But, why was this problem not anticipated? How is mismanagement of something as fundamental as food allowed to occur?

Our challenges don't stop there; there is crime driven by narcotic addiction whilst other addictive substances with proven harmful effects, like cigarettes, are sold to children in third world countries at prices often cheaper than the nourishment they need to sustain their growing bodies – all motivated by the need to make profit. There is on-going harm to animals, landscape and climate whilst our leaders disagree on action and make decisions based on short-term revenues and convenience rather than the fact that the planet and humankind face disaster unless the issue is dealt with swiftly.

The failure of key countries to adopt the Kyoto Protocol or to come to meaningful agreement in Copenhagen (which was intended to institute emissions reduction targets) indicates the priorities of our Governments. Other environmental agreements may be made and signed in future but can we depend on all signatories and nations to abide by the spirit and the letter of the pact, rather than seek commercial advantage by breaking the terms. But our political leaders will defend their stance by pointing to the industries, profits and jobs they are defending by ignoring the climate change issue. They will say they are balancing jobs against environmental damage; trying to find compromise between the need for profits, employment and the needs of the planet. Despite the inaction and lip service to action, our leaders still find new and innovative ways of taxing the people under the 'green' banner.

Meanwhile, some religious leaders compound the turmoil by infecting those they influence with fear, and hatred for those that express their spiritual beliefs differently. They magnify the minor differences to justify war and the theft of resources, often appealing to God to support amazing cruelties, offering prayers and blessings to the slaughter of other peoples, whilst promising its followers rewards in the hereafter. Even those religious leaders that speak out against war do so whilst providing Chaplains to the combatants, who do not tell the soldiers to put the weapons down.

All of these events have two things in common: the division of humankind into groups and sub-groups. These groups are then encouraged to fight, murder, war, steal, lie, cheat, defame others and debase their own humanity and not recognise the humanity of another, often over resources thought to be in short supply. People are made to compete and war like the birds of a cock-fight, which never realise that their death serves only as entertainment to their oppressors who remain untouched by it all. The second thing in common is that someone, somewhere always profits from the misery and therefore has no incentive to prevent it.

Unlike those poor birds we can review our situation and chose a different path, but first we have to recognise both the oppression and our strength.

With apologies for mixing metaphors or imagery, it takes two

4

dogs and a shepherd to control a flock of sheep. This can only happen with the submissive acceptance of the sheep. The sheep have the power but the shepherd has control.

What if the sheep said 'no more'?

A few may get bitten, but if we discovered our solidarity, the dogs could not prevail.

This is not about fixing our money based economy, it is about replacing it with an economy that deals with the problems of all humans; not one excluded. This book will introduce you to a very old idea that is ripe for modernisation and more importantly tell you why our money based way of distributing goods and services will inevitably fail and why the problems we face are inevitable. The poverty, crime, warfare, hunger, disregard for humanity and the excessive privilege of a few we see around us is rooted in the failing logic of money and although it is all clearly dysfunctional, it is inevitable until we change the world order and bring true peace, prosperity and security to all. Our current way of distributing resources and making group decisions is clearly not addressing human issues.

It is tough but we can change it all. There is an alternative and we, the people, can make it happen.

Book One: Where We Are

I

The Current Financial System

A dictatorship would be a heck of a lot easier, there's no doubt about it.

G.W Bush

What is Money? Why does it exist? Is it real?

Money is anything that people will accept as payment or compensation for goods and services provided and the satisfaction of debts, meaning that people must agree on its value and have confidence in it for it to be accepted. It is used as a medium of exchange, a unit of account thus allowing relative worth to be easily established and compared (i.e. each product or item is designated with a value in currency – so we know to pay less for a common pebble than a gold nugget). Money is also a store of value which can be saved (where it is useful for its potential purchasing power) and reliably retrieved when it is required as a medium of exchange.

Money now has several guises. We have banknotes and coins in circulation, but the bulk of money is now electronic, meaning it changes hands by computer ledger entries, via mediums such as credit and debit cards, cheques and other signifiers of money such as bonds, etc.

The origins of money are truly ancient. Records are inconclusive but money and currency date back at least to 4,000 years before the birth of Christ with the Sumer civilization of Mesopotamia and there is some evidence that money was used in Swaziland 100,000 years ago. During the development of money – cattle, whale teeth, jewellery, shells, salt and tobacco have been used as currency. Fundamentally, anything that society would accept as rare and suitable in satisfying the requisites of money. These items were often exchanged for items of subsistence in its earliest days. Prior to money people bartered to exchange needed resources. However, distributing goods in this manner is hopelessly ineffective at satisfying needs due to the problem of finding an individual with a surplus of what you need, who is also prepared to accept something you can offer – a double coincidence of wants is needed.

Trade or exchanging goods and services between people forced the development of the early markets and currency to ease the process of trading – hence money is often referred to as 'liquidity' in financial circles.

It is important however, to note the type of society and the level of sophistication that gave birth to the idea of money as an aid to trade.

Basically, money was a development intended to address the problems of a subsistence level, low technology, and low resource society which had to quickly develop an effective rationing and distribution mechanism. It was a way of exchanging scarce resources for those with unequal access to the necessities of life. It had the effect of ensuring that those with higher social status retained first pick of what was available (these high status people being the controllers of the rationing mechanism), rather than there being a disorderly scramble. It served the function of maintaining social order when stability was under strain and cementing the authority and status of those that controlled the supply and availability of money and with that all food, goods, services and labour.

If all people had equal access to the necessities of life and there were no shortages, it would not have been necessary to develop barter, trade and money as a means of rationing. Imagine a small medieval village where the weather is always temperate. The surroundings are blessed with an abundance of clean fresh water, food crops, fruit and nuts that need no cultivation and which are available all year round. Further to that, cattle is easily available to amply feed the residents. If all the residents had access to everything there is clearly no absolute need for exchange or barter and no need to steal from each other or raid the neighbouring villages. Specialisations of labour would likely develop as individuals selected the tasks they preferred, which would encourage cooperation among the villagers. But the abundance around the villagers would negate the need to develop a mechanism of exchange, because everything important is available to each individual. A significant affect of this abundance is to reduce the ability or incentive of any individual to impose his will on another person or force unwilling compliance. There would be no means for a small social elite to achieve authority and power over a community of self-sufficient and independent people; they have everything they could want and can only be physically threatened. To further illustrate this important point, now imagine this village suffers an event that restricts the food available.

It is likely that certain individuals would scheme to assure themselves of priority access and consume more than they would equitably be entitled to, under the guise of minimising the impact of the new shortages on the group. Additionally, when abundance did return it is unlikely these individuals would voluntarily relinquish their new found position of power; even if it was harming others and no longer necessary.

You can deduce from this that scarcity breeds hierarchy, because scarcity generates the need for people to maintain social order by developing an acceptable method of rationing. This rationing causes unequal access to resources, which in turn guarantees that a few will seek control and gain access to everything they need (and more), while the rest experience shortage; that fortunate few will also benefit from disproportionate power of influence, respect and patronage – hierarchy. They will achieve an artificially high social status purely because they have the power to dispense and deny access to needed resources.

For the ancient people, money was an ingenious way of managing scarce resources in a society where each individual and group has to live, die or prosper by their own efforts. Money was their best way of avoiding unrelenting squabbling with neighbours caused by insufficient resources and allowed some individuals to elevate the importance of their contribution to society above that of another. However, the impact on the majority of people for a higher chance of personal survival was to accept their subordinate place in society and accept the authority of others over them. This submission was the only way to gain an opportunity to receive something from the rationing process; any person that refused to cooperate found themselves outside of the system, persecuted and unable to meet their human needs. Comply or starve.

Indications are that in the early days of money, it was the resources represented that were important not the currency itself; even today we cannot eat money – it must be exchanged for something useful. However, it was, and still is important to have access to a reliable supply of money, because it acts as a barrier between what we need and what we get.

As time passes and society moves from subsistence living,[3] yet does nothing to modernise the means of distributing needed resources. The outdated money mechanism now evolves from assisting the survival of various groups and maintaining group order into an instrument of control within the groups of people. This is achieved through a despotic process and taxation. The individual holding money (or introducing it) has control over society since people must obey them to earn some of that money and therefore have an opportunity to feed themselves. Let us briefly look at this: Our legal systems often use a process of cash confiscation, to control, curb or manage our behaviours. Conversely, if the authorities wish to encourage an activity, we are offered financial reward. In combination, the ability to grant and deny access to money bestows huge influence over an entire population. Mayer Amschel Rothschild, European Central Banker (1744 – 1812) said it best, "Give me control of a nation's money and I care not who makes the laws."

In addition, the principal of taxation means that people must work a portion of their time in order to pay a government, monarchy or individual who uses that income for whatever purpose they choose, without input from the person making the payments. Even now, we have no influence over how our taxes are used, whether it's to fund wars of acquisition or allow banking institutions to pay generous bonuses to its staff. Any individual that attempts to withhold payment of tax faces loss of liberty and being made an example of.

Income taxation was introduced in the UK and America to allow leaders to pay the wages of soldiers, who were then used for personal security, maintenance of social order, and acquisition of further resources through war, either from neighbouring territories or less well armed wealthy individuals.[4] The existence of a militia has meant throughout history that the population could now be forced to pay tribute and that the commodities for survival (such as land, water etc) could be controlled and owned by one individual, who often claimed special association with God and/or used this heightened status to institute a dynastic and hereditary structure that protected the privileges of that family, often becoming royalty. With the entrancement of money and its host society increasing sophistication, banking as an institution becomes inevitable.

The Egypt that built the pyramids is reputed to have developed the first simple banks; they had some fantastic achievements but social equality was not one of them. The first banks we would recognise as practicing near modern principals came later with the Knights Templar and were safekeeping depositories where depositors kept items of value for which they received a note from the bank as a receipt. As confidence grew in the banks, these bank notes were used as goods in trade since the bank notes represented a real asset that could be reclaimed upon presentation of the note to the issuing bank. It wasn't long before the bankers realised that the depositors rarely redeemed all of their notes at the same time which allowed the banks to lend other people's money because they often had depositors gold gathering dust in their vaults. They found they could charge interest in order to make an income from nowhere, even through some cultures had anti-usury customs. The banks no longer just took fees for providing depositor services and a safe-hold; they found themselves receiving interest income from gold deposited with them, eventually lending more money than the value of assets they held, receiving interest on money they did not have in the first place.

The power to issue loans (creating money from nowhere) conveyed huge powers and influence upon the banks. Bankers found themselves at the pinnacle of social influence, being able to control those around them simply by withholding or dispensing money. The influence money confers has profound consequences.

Money Grants Control Over Groups

Money can only be used to control groups when survival of the whole group is no longer an issue, and group members can be made to feel that money is essential to the survival of the individual within the group. No individual wants to perish so this is simply achieved by placing a money value on everything that is important to human survival. To illustrate Mayer Rothschild's point, imagine that you walk past an apple tree every day and habitually take an apple for free and you have grown accustomed to that treat. However, on your next walk it has been fenced off and someone is now demanding a token of payment in exchange for your regular apple. You have the choice now of whether you go without or if you submit yourself to labour in order to earn the token you must now exchange for it. Now imagine that the person demanding payment is backed up by a military group who assume control of everything you need to survive and demands payment before they allow you access. Now, compound that with there being only a few places you can earn the cash you suddenly need. You find yourself doing something you don't want to do, for a token you don't need so you can swap that for something you do want. The illusionary nature of money is starting to become clear because you only ever wanted the apple, and the apple is still there but now you need to submit to someone to earn a token to exchange for it. In fact, to be selected for employment you now need to demonstrate yourself to be more submissive and useful than the other applicants. The unsuccessful applicants get nothing and the successful live in fear of losing their position. Of course the above is a simplification, but it is clear there is a cost for the social order and the management of apparently scarce supplies. The cost is disregard for individual human need, the potential for abuse of individuals as they scrabble for tokens and disproportionate power to those that control the currency.

Let's briefly justify this contention using economic theory.

In accepted economic theory there are four resources that are necessary to satisfy human needs: land, labour, entrepreneurship and capital; to this list I would like to add knowledge or "technical know-how". Basically, to satisfy the demands of society there has to be an entrepreneur or risk taker/organiser to coordinate land and/or property, workers and money to pay for everything. And as the demands of society become more sophisticated, the use of technology and scientific knowledge must be included in the economic mix to convert raw earth resources into something that satisfies society's demands.

In our current system, it is impossible to attract labour, land and resource coordinators without money. Therefore, an entrepreneur with access to a factory but without money cannot achieve anything, regardless how needed his produce is, whereas someone holding capital can acquire whatever they want and create whatever they want regardless of the interests of labour, land and the wider society – capital out ranks it all.

Therefore the interests of capital have priority over everything else. Before Rothschild, the Egyptians were first to realise that whoever controls the wealth controls the group. They were well-versed in designing rigid social structures and using violence to enforce it. They failed to realise that more effective and self-sustaining control could be achieved by manipulating and distributing valueless symbols and tokens that represent wealth and then restricting access to the resources needed to sustain life.

So what does this mean to us?

The principals of money management and manipulation (and the control it bestows) have changed very little since the days of the Knights Templar's banking services, and the impact has not changed at all.[5] Naturally, present methods and techniques have become more sophisticated but an Egyptian scribe and Templar banker would actually recognise the intent and results of our current financial practice and our social structures. That scribe would immediately see that the pyramidal social structure still prevails with a few individuals, families or institutions holding sway over the mass of people, the key difference being that control is exerted by fear of lack of money rather than fear of the whip. He would recognise that replacing the obvious cruelty with the subtlety of illusionary money would create a society just as cruel but infinitely easier to control because the slaves themselves would see no reason to revolt or run away, and would deny themselves the means to revolt. In fact, if the controllers of money managed the situation correctly they would have the benefits of a slave system with none of the downside; the people wouldn't recognise their status, and would be mostly self -policing.

A brief review of history shows us how little things have changed. The Egyptians (approximately 2,500 BC) used slave labour to create huge structures that only a few benefited from. As a people they had access to knowledge, skills and wealth that amaze us today, but the bounty of that society was available only to a very select few, on the backs of the many that suffered to provide it.

It is understood that the Egyptian slavers had no other intent than providing the barest subsistence levels of food and shelter in forced exchange for their labour. It is clear that discipline among workers was problematic, causing a relatively high number of supervisors needed to whip the labour force into action and the slaves needed to be constantly replaced through deaths and the tendency of slaves to run away – a very wasteful process. The beneficiaries of this labour were a tiny social elite regarded as God-like.

Fast forward approximately 3,900 years, to the 1600's AD; inter-related Royal families have replaced Pharaohs and money is now adopted in Europe. The European world finds itself with a problem of how to provide products to its needy people at an artificially low price. Years of British political civil war and religious conflict in mainland Europe created social unrest among the poor in particular who were agitating against the unfair distribution of resources. There were nonconformist dissenting groups [6] that were threatening the cohesion of society and again social discipline was problematic for the elite.

Government is forced to find a way of improving the standard of living of the poor to win back their compliance, whilst not diluting any of their own wealth, power and influence. They needed a way of making a meaningless concession to the mass of their people without risking any change that addressed the real issue of the majority of people being excluded from the benefits of a financial system. Even when efforts are made to alleviate the suffering of people in a money system it takes a rare individual to ignore an opportunity for personal gain. In fact, in a money economy, those in a position to help people have an incentive not to do so unless it can be done whilst improving their own personal status. It is simply logical to just give the appearance of helping or find someone else to pay.

The Cruel Logic of Money

Under our money system there is only one logical answer, make someone else pay regardless of how. Everything in a monetary system, including people, is reduced to the status of commodity with no consideration for anything other than profit. Because the church would share the bounty and win converts, the church supported the abduction of millions of slaves and salved the conscience of the slavers (with stories of God's curse on black people), whilst their victims were transported to the Caribbean and the Americas. The real payers were forced to labour in inhumane conditions to benefit the corporation owners and, indirectly, European society. Once the slave could not work, they were often disposed of. There are accounts of slaves being killed when auctions went poorly and it was considered too expensive to feed and maintain an unwanted slave. This was how the establishment chose to solve the problem of a restless domestic population. Naturally, the benefits of slavery only helped the home population by allowing it to be possible to survive. While the slavers had priority access to the proceeds and became super rich, there is an argument that those slaver families are still benefiting today.

This cannot be said to be a purely racial or ultimately evil thing, it is the logic of money cruelly applied. In a money society someone must always pay; the Japanese enslaved the Koreans, the Jews were reportedly enslaved by the Egyptians and later the Nazi's, there was slavery in the Islamic Caliphate, within the Roman Empire, within Eastern Europe, with the Cossacks and this ancient brutality still exists today. This has always been and remains today. People are enslaved and the benefits of that slavery are used to help the population of the beneficiary nation to maintain a subsistence-plus lifestyle of relative comfort; whilst the slavers themselves receive huge profit. The population of the benefiting nation is kept unaware of how their standard of living is achieved/supported by the suffering of unseen peoples and the status quo rolls on. But even the beneficiary population have problems in a money system.

The British working classes also suffered during the Industrial Revolution.[7] People were lured from the land with the prospect of money and when they were unable to work (through sickness, industrial injuries or redundancy) were left to starve or turn to crime. Many were deported to Australia or the Slave Colonies to labour for the few at the top of the pyramid. Under a money system even those close to home are reduced to the status of a commodity – again a few dynastic families and institutions benefit and the workers are discarded after their useful years have passed.

Now it is estimated that 27 million people throughout the world (including children)[8] are now enslaved – some by suppliers of companies we know very well. Anti Slavery International reports on concerns, interventions and legal action against Burger King, Taco Bell, The Chocolate Manufacturers of America, Primark and others.

The West is benefiting from these activities yet we have so many problems of our own. It is only the owners of these corporations that truly cash in whilst our daily struggles to pay bills continue.

With this still happening it is easy to see why the West can still be described as predatory and imperialist and why we are still deeply unpopular in certain countries and subject to terrorist action, yet it is not the people of the West that truly benefit or indeed cause the suffering of others.

And for the majority, who are not directly enslaved, let's look at the circumstances of our lives:

We exchange our time for money at a task we may or may not enjoy; this is called gainful employment. The money received is never enough because it is as little as the employer can get away with to pay taxes (usually paid first), accommodation and food. We often work 40 years at the end of which we are only tired, broke, not always with a guaranteed adequate pension and the money we are able to save is subject to tax and inflation. We are now discarded to fend for ourselves just as any slave was hundreds of years ago, uncertain that we will have access to the bounty that surrounds us and meet our needs.

Because we don't think there's any other way, and have nowhere to run, we content ourselves with a bit of time off now and then and polite treatment from our employers. We stick at the task, whilst the corporation prospers, because we don't recognise our options.

Even the peoples in the 'free' and prosperous countries are suffering under our economic system whilst those from poorer nations have the worst possible deal. In prosperous Britain a recent survey by Birmingham Midshires Building Society reported that the average adult had £2,000 saved. This average allows for the 9 million adults with no savings and the wealthy. In the world's most powerful nation, a Temple University survey found 30% of American adults have less than $1,000 and 50% less than $10,000. Not nearly enough in either country to provide any form of security, again there is good economic reason for this that is discussed later. In the Democratic Republic of Congo, two thirds of the entire population is malnourished and many survive by hunting and eating bush-meat, often chimpanzees and gorillas.

Why does this continue? Why is it that intelligent humankind has been unable to solve the simple matter of caring for our own and our environment? Our current system is clearly failing us, yet no-one does anything to change it.

2

Four Thousand Years of Progress but No Real Change

In the absence of the gold standard, there is no way to protect savings from confiscation through inflation; there is no safe store of value.

Alan Greenspan, Ex Chairman
– Federal Reserve of America.

Why has money and society changed so little over the centuries? No doubt technology has improved, becoming more effective and efficient at meeting our increasingly sophisticated needs, yet the societies we have are effectively unchanged from the rigid hieratical structures of old with few enjoying bounty and the majority struggling to have their needs met or at least regularly experiencing resource insecurity.

The answer is so very simple, but first we have to understand the current economic system.

The banknote in your pocket was printed and issued upon the order of central Government. The Government issued a Treasury Bond (essentially an I.O.U.) which was created with a repayment date and interest due to be paid at that date. The bond is issued principally to The Bank of England in the UK (State owned since 1946, and the privately owned Federal Reserve in America, which by law is not subject to audit).[9] These institutions then print the cash the bond represents (less profit) and deliver it to the government's nominated banks – this becomes part of the recipient bank's capital reserve holding.

In a process called 'Fractional Reserve Banking'[10] the banks holding this money, created from a government debt document, are allowed to lend a proportion to other banks, who are themselves permitted to lend to other banks, corporations and individuals. This means that when £100 is deposited with a bank, that deposit is actually worth up to £1,000 of issued loans and the accruing interest on £1,000 to the banking system.

Banks were originally required to hold substantial reserves to guarantee the stability of the banking system and it has been the erosion of the principal of holding substantial reserves that has contributed to the recent banking crisis. The reserve requirement has proven to be a useful mechanism for controlling the money supply and with that, the availability of money to people. Suppose the reserve requirement is 10 percent of deposits. The following chart shows effect of £/$100 deposited into Bank A.

Deposits Reserves Loans
Bank A 100 10 90
Lends to...
Bank B 90 9 81
Lends to...
Bank C 81 8.10 72.90
Lends to...
Bank D 72.90 7.29 65.61
Lends to...
Bank E 65.61 6.56 59.05
Lends to...
Bank F 59.05 5.90 53.15
Lends to...
Bank G 53.15 5.31 47.84
Lends to...
Bank H 47.84 4.78 43.06
Lends to...
Bank I 43.06 4.30 38.76
Lends to...

Bank J 38.76 3.87 34.89
Etc...

The total lent is £586.26 when only £100 was created.

This chart illustrates that when a state creates £/$100 of cash at interest. The banking system quickly turns that cash into loans that suddenly generates huge income streams from lending money that never really existed.

This process has been adopted worldwide since the abandonment of the Gold Standard.[11] As the population grew; the gold standard was abandoned because money backed by gold restricted the amount of money in circulation. A lack of money is dangerous to an economy because it becomes impossible to pay for goods and services and the system grinds to a halt.

This indicates why confidence is a word so often used when discussing our economy; confidence is the most substantial element to it. Our economy needs confidence because our currency is not pegged to anything of substance and it has value purely because we are prepared to accept it. This also explains why gold prices rocket during a recession; the investors know there is a possibility that confidence in a currency may expire (leaving them holding a valueless currency) whilst confidence in gold is eternal. During this banking crisis there has been a marked increase in gold purchasing advertising, basically those that are able are exchanging risky currency for something with intrinsic valve, leaving those unable to do so exposed. An excellent illustration of why confidence is the most substantial part of a money economy is the anatomy of a recession. A recession is defined as a significant decline in economic activity spread across the economy which lasts more than a few months. In practical terms that reduction in economic activity results in business failures, loan defaults, unemployment, increased homelessness and generally less money available to meet the needs of a population.

The increase in unemployment means people have less money to spend and the money available needs to be used with great caution, thus discretionary spending such as holidays, etc is curtailed. It appears as if money simply disappears and this is what we are conditioned to believe. In reality most of the money never actually existed. We mostly made purchases in the expectation that we would receive a salary or other payment that will allow us to meet our commitments. The confidence in our ability to pay at a future date kept us spending and the economy buoyant. We bought houses, cars and other major purchases in the expectation of being able to pay. In effect we spent our money before we received it. If however we have reason to lose confidence in our financial future, it is necessary for us to cut all discretionary spending to protect ourselves from the unpleasant anticipated event. The economy finds itself in a vicious cycle, where a lack of personal confidence translates into reduced personal spending, which means reduced income for others and the spiral continues.

Having established that a significant component of a recession is an individual's personal assessment of their ability to pay in the future, multiplied by the numbers that share that pessimistic sentiment, it's appropriate to follow where the available money goes.

During a recession those that have money save it prudently at their banks, generally avoiding investment opportunities because the risk of investment failure is perceived to be high (thus removing it from circulation) and those without money have their possessions and property reclaimed by the banks if they find themselves unable to service debt. Either way the money that is available ends up in the hands of the few bank owners and they decide how to distribute it.

Only a small proportion of money is available in note or coin form.[12] This means that most money does not even physically exist; it is only a ledger entry on a bank's computer, which allows all transactions to be monitored, logged and recorded. This lack of physical money confers further power of control to the banking system because transactions increasingly must be conducted through them and no longer person to person. Our financial system is entirely a phantom.

Just to make our situation absolutely clear. The banks lend money created from nothing, while we repay them with our labour and sweat AND reward them with interest (additional labour) on the money that never existed in the first place. The illusionary nature of money is obvious because its value is set not by resources balanced against demand or our labour – it is set by the institutions that issue and trade our debt, which is why mistakes made in our banking institutions can cripple the whole world real economy, where real products and services are provided and people find employment.

Coming away from the gold standard and increasing the money supply also encourages inflation. Inflation robs the saver of the purchasing power they have accumulated and the saver has absolutely no control over it's affect, but banks and governments do by the issuance or restriction of Treasury Bonds (and other financial instruments) and the availability of bank credit. Inflation can reward the reckless borrower because he repays his debt with cheaper money than he borrowed, for example if I had borrowed £100 from you 25 years ago and repay you today, you would find that it would only have the value of £41.15 because of inflation. This has a huge negative impact on those prudently saving for retirement or major purchases. It's the same for virtually all currencies. We find ourselves with an economy with no substance where prudent behaviour is often punished and only a small elite knows and controls what will happen next with the value of the money we work for.

There are two essential points about Fractional Banking. If we all tried to get our savings back most of us would lose everything because the bank does not have it and there can NEVER be enough money to satisfy the debt in the system because that debt was created from nothing and the application of interest compounds the issue further.

This means that in a money system there must be winners and losers: people getting richer and others with nothing because there isn't enough money in the system to satisfy the debt, therefore repaying with interest obliges the borrower to extract excess funds from those he deals with thus reducing their ability to meet their human needs. Meanwhile, well paid professions or those that provide essential human services at profit further reduce the monies available to everyone else. This problem exists regardless of whether a government has left or right sympathies because the problem is the money around which every decision is made. The banknote in your pocket represents someone's debt. In England our banknotes are a promise from the Bank of England to pay the bearer in gold; the insidious impact of this is that over time tangible assets, such as property, slowly moves from the hands of the public to the ownership of those that own the banks. The banking sector has mortgages on approximately 54 per cent of UK housing stock, and 68 per cent in the US. This movement of valuable assets up the societal pyramid happens because even in the best economic times there are people unable to keep up with their debt commitments and the lending bank forecloses or repossesses (with the defaulter still liable to pay for the outstanding debt in the UK). The bank then resells that same property with debt money created from nothing to another hopeful home-buyer. As time passes more people are stripped of what they have worked hard for and are still forced to exchange labour for the ability to house and feed themselves and their families.

There is also an important impact upon people that cannot be forgotten. Debt for essential items such as a home keeps people submissive and easily managed by the few that hold this illusionary commodity we have been made to feel we need. This stops us from ever feeling secure and distracting us from dealing with the root of our problems.

To illustrate this point further, the advent of compound interest has done more to keep people working and unable to provide financial security than anything else. Einstein said 'The most powerful force in the universe is compound interest' and '(compound interest is) the greatest invention in human history'. A typical home loan will require the borrower to repay a multiple of the amount actually borrowed over the course of 25-30 years; the bulk of monthly payments are made purely to service interest on the debt, which was created from nothing in the first place. For example, a loan of £100,000 with a modest interest rate of 4 per cent would cost £158,349 over 25 years and £171,867 over 30 years.

We effectively exchange 30 years of labour for the means to acquire a home and during that time we remain fearful that we may lose the opportunity to labour, because that means homelessness. Therefore, a working family can rent a property and pay until the day they die or they can devote many years of their lives working to own their home and during that time they are dependent on the goodwill of their employer or if self-employed, their clients because the alternative would be too horrible to contemplate. Any interruption during that working life could spell disaster, additionally the individual is dependent on the government's and bank's management of the economy because a mistake or action taken by them can destroy the plans of the most prudent and hardworking. The despotism is clear to see. The Egyptian scribe would be pleased to see that our society has achieved his aims without all the tiresome whipping and runaway slaves. The only thing that would surprise him would be that people are willing to slave for a token which has no intrinsic value and that we willingly turn up to please our employer without a whip, he would also be surprised to see that we confuse worthless tokens for the resources we need.

Do we have so much collective Stockholm syndrome that we are prepared to prop up a despotic system that abuses us?

3

The Impact of Money on Society

I believe that banking institutions are more dangerous to our liberties than standing armies. If the American people ever allow private banks to control the issue of their currency, first by inflation, the banks and corporations that will grow up around (the banks) will deprive the people of all property until their children wake up homeless on the continent their fathers conquered.

Thomas Jefferson

Money was an ingenious solution to problems that no longer existed once human kind had passed the risk of species extinction. The use, manipulation and management of money became more sophisticated as society evolved (ie company shares, bonds and other complex financial instruments) whilst the intent behind money did not. The power of the bank grew as more people and the less well-off had reason to deal with those institutions and like any institution its first priority is to the survival of itself. The banking system helped in the creation of an entire class of individuals who owe their prosperity not to the creation of goods and services but to their ability to deal with intangible transactions.[13]

These financial management related jobs are currently well paid and most support the despotic process already discussed. The language these professions use is designed to complicate and obscure; thus discouraging many amateurs from understanding the simple processes that are happening.

The biggest single development in society, which placed the banking system at the pinnacle of human affairs, was the advent of profit.

Profit is the increase in wealth that an investor or business owner creates after taking all costs into account. It is reward for an economic activity and often has an inverse relationship to risk. It is also used as the key measure of success for any economic activity and is the sole true objective of any business or corporate activity.

Profit also divided people into two groups: the investor/business owners (typically politically right wing), and labour (typically politically left wing). This book is non political and the above comment is intended as description/observation only. However, these distinctions serve as a divider of people – one group or class seeking to protect their portion from the jealousy of those less privileged. The dividing of people is a natural consequence of an economy based upon money. It is the logic of money. It is also logical that the few that benefit from the economic confidence trick that we live under will use any means to distract us from recognising what is really going on.

Money also has an impact on how we deal with the problems common to every human on this planet. Every human is born naked, in need of clothes, regular food, toilet facilities, a warm place to live, protection, company, education, entertainment and healthcare. Money addresses these needs but in an ineffective, wasteful and often cruel way. Businesses provide these services for profit and profit is the prime indicator of success rather than the satisfaction of human need. This means that the business that provides quality goods and services by well-rewarded and cared for staff is likely to be less successful then the organisation that cuts corners and extracts the highest possible labour with lowest possible compensation. We see example after example of businesses that purport to provide human services but, in the pursuit of profit, actually harm us. Let's take a look at this.

The Food Industry

In order to provide us with cheap food, animals can be kept and transported in the most appalling conditions, fed hormones to force unnaturally large and speedy growth and fed the corpses of their kin to reduce the cost of rearing the animal. We are provided with a cheaper than ethically possible meal and the supplier enjoys a large profit margin.

However, when we purchase that meat, not only are we supporting the cruelty, we are endangering our own long-term health by ingesting the chemicals, etc, forced upon that animal. But of course we are prepared to ignore these issues because we cannot afford to be ethical on our limited money budget and we hope the health issues[14] won't happen to us anyway. We feel we have no choice but to support the cruelty even if we find it distasteful, because the same meal respectfully/ethically reared can cost several times as much as the cruel meal and we have difficult choices to make with our limited money. The fact that the producers of ethically reared meat go out of business or are forced to become 'cheap producers' too is just a sad consequence of the profit driven system. But, the real irony is that the false popularity of the cheap meat producer will actually allow him to increase his prices and his profits after the respectful/ethical producer has gone, so we end up with the thing we didn't really want, at a higher cost and fewer options.

It is a similar process with our grains and vegetables. Farmers are under pressure to be cheap producers, so they spray their crop with pesticides and chemicals to keep insects away and make intensive short-term use of land and labour. The affects of this is that unintended victims such as bees and other insect life are severely impacted upon. The farm workers themselves are experiencing problems[15] and we who ingest those chemicals can experience serious health issues such as ME, CJD etc. and other nerve damage issues, which did not have a significant presence until our farming practices were 'modernised' and became more financially efficient.

That's not the end of it. Because of the pressure for profit and the drive to find the cheapest solution possible, regardless of the impact, we are forced into accepting Genetically Modified Foods. These are crops adjusted at genetic level to make them resistant or unattractive to insects and disease. We are doing this because it is cheaper than using more land for agriculture and growing food naturally and healthily, or using other innovative methods to address our problems.

Naturopathic physician Christopher Pick N.D advises that the medical establishment is aware that the human body requires around 70 minerals, 16 vitamins, 12 essential amino acids, three essential fatty acids and around two litres of fresh, chemical-free water each day, combined with appropriate exercise and rest for optimal health, vitality and longevity. We would get these in a well-balanced organic diet. But no meaningful attempt is made to provide our bodies with what we need. Indeed, our General Medical Practitioners are provided with minimal training in the importance of nutritional factors.

We are advised that there is no cause for concern about GM foods and indeed certain groups have described them as absolutely safe and a solution to looming food shortage problems.[16] However, in May 2005, a major proponent and maker of GM foods (Monsanto) fed their own rats on MON863 strain of GM corn for only 90 days and found that there were changes in kidney size and blood composition. When this information was brought to the attention of the European Food and Safety Authority (E.F.S.A.) they concluded that the changes were biologically insignificant and MON863 was approved for human and animal consumption. We are eating MON863 now without an understanding of the longer term impact.[17] In America GM Foods have escaped the need to be safety tested or indeed labelled.[18] This is probably another public health emergency (like CJD) in the waiting.

Events like these are not isolated. Posilac (or rBST) is a genet-ically engineered hormone fed to cows to increase milk yields; unfortunately it makes many cows sick. It was banned in Europe but Monsanto Corporation launched and won a legal battle to force its acceptance on the grounds of there being no incontro-vertible evidence of harm to humans.[19] We are drinking it now in Europe, America and other places (mostly without labelling) but it is banned in Canada because of its potential for human health problems.

In a money system it makes financial sense to behave so irresponsibly and put off the health concerns of others to some unspecified date. At the time the health problems arise, there will be another shortcut or minor compensation payment made at a fraction of the profits made or indeed no absolutely conclusive evidence that the product is responsible for the problems that people experience.

The smoking industry did just that and spent many years defending their product despite mounting evidence (the deaths and sickness of many of their customers) before finally being forced to concede there may be a health concern. Even with that evidence firmly established, the power of that industry allows them to seek new markets and new profit centres. It is the logic of our money system that they continue to allow people to painfully poison themselves (and others) until the last possible moment and when people try to finally make that industry accountable; they'll simply close shop and file for legal protection.

Another example is the pharmaceutical/health industry. There are examples of drug companies trying to have long established herbal remedies restricted or removed to allow expensively developed drugs to be unopposed and achieve higher profit (St John's Wort is an example of this which will be replaced by tranquilisers should the legal action be successful). Where it is not possible to remove competition from herbal remedies, the pharmaceutical corporations simply buy the herbalist firms.[20] This allows the pharmaceutical firms to control their competitors and therefore decide the efficacy of the herbal treatments. They will control the result of comparative testing. In what way does this help the consumer?

Worst still, there are several examples of pharmaceutical firms that have released drugs known to be tainted into the third world or other markets, because they felt it was cheaper to pay small compensation claims than not harm anyone. Destroying the dangerous drug and protecting people from it after their expensive development processes was simply too expensive to consider, regardless of the human cost. This is exactly what happened when Haemophiliacs were dying from treatments tainted with HIV.[21] There are other examples of similar practices including drugs exported from Puerto Rico into America.

The profit motive has lead to several examples of drugs being rushed to sale without thorough understanding of the side effects, or being used after the discovery of a more effective option because the original drug has not yet paid back its investment. Children have been born deformed and people have died but the Corporations use lawyers to avoid or reduce their culpability and protect their profits.[22] This is simply good business practice.

In this profit driven society, what incentive is there to find a cure for the common cold when so much profit is made year after year from us buying treatments that mask the symptoms rather than cure us?

Even in our popular drinks and foods today there are unsafe ingredients such as Aspartame that create real health problems. Aspartame was refused a food license for many years because it caused brain cancer in rats and the American Food and Drug Administration published a report in the 1980's noting 91 other side affects. It was developed to be an anti-ulcer drug, but was accidentally discovered to taste sweet. Because there is bigger profit potential in a low calorie sweetener this 'medicine' was re-branded as a food helpful as part of a calorie controlled diet to aid slimming and became a huge financial success, despite the fact it is linked with so many serious health conditions. It is rumoured that the only reason Aspartame was granted a food license is because a senior member of the Bush Administration (Donald Rumsfeld) is one of the owners of the patent.

If Aspartame is stored incorrectly or for too long,[23] it breaks down into a compound extremely hazardous to health, yet it is an ingredient in more than 6,000 very popular foods, sweets and drinks. Ironically, this ingredient is also found in children's vitamin supplements. No caring drinks and food provider would make us ingest these ingredients but for the profit they receive; and we are encouraged to give these to our *children* through attractive advertising and little gifts. The final insult is the advertising tells us it is good for us because it helps us manage our weight.[23]

This tendency of commercial companies to ignore human concerns is exacerbated by the drive to achieve profits quickly, so innovations that could transform and improve the human experience of life will be suppressed or pass away without interest unless there is a way to charge money for it or charge for maintenance of it and make a profit quickly. A good example of this is built-in or planned obsolescence of so many of our appliances, [24] forcing us to continually replace them. It is said that the patent for an ever-lasting light bulb is held by a major corporation that wishes to charge us for continual replacements. If profit cannot be made quickly the project is doomed to failure regardless of how excellent it may be. Another problem is the money system requires any new innovation/invention (unless it is the creation of someone with personal resources) to be filtered through the establishment. Any new idea needs money to have a chance of benefiting humankind. To get the money it is necessary to get the approval and funding of a bank or corporation (they require a quick profit or a personal guarantee, usually the inventors home), but these few institutions decide what idea they back and they do so after filtering through their own vested interests. Even this book went through the same process of rejection from publishers with a vested interest, some were subsidiaries of the corporations mentioned later in this book. Therefore, the existence of money acts as a drain and impediment to human development, in addition to supporting an artificial hierarchy. Not only is money not addressing the concerns of humanity, it is now actually harming us.

For example, in the mid 1970's Vittorio Sorgato of Milan, Italy developed a compressed air-powered car which the industry was not interested in. Stanley Meyer, in the 1990's, developed a water (hydrogen) powered car; he died shortly after he demonstrated it working.[25] It is only now that overwhelming evidence for global warming is existent that the fossil fuel industries are being forced to accept a declining role.

In a world where the pursuit of profit is paramount, the needs of people are easily ignored and we (the victims) continually fail to act; we accept it and put it to the back of our minds. After all, it was not me or mine that was hurt this time and we feel there is nothing we personally can do.

We live in a world where 1 per cent of the US Government's defence budget would feed the world[26] and entirely abolish hunger but that isn't on the agenda of the few that can make it happen and we do not fight for it. We are too busy competing for money and inadvertently supporting the few people that make these awful decisions. We live in a world were people starve while the wealthier nations have, until recently, stockpiled or destroyed food in order to maintain artificially high prices, and because we are all so busy dealing with our own personal problems, nothing changes and more people get hurt. To add insult to injury there are highly secretive cash and investment funds (called Sovereign Wealth Funds) held by states and individuals (many from the oil rich countries) that have access to US$14.7 trillion (or US$ 14,700,000,000,000) enough to solve every problem this world faces.[27] But all it does is accrue more interest for its owners (typically received from taxing the populations of debtor nations) and consolidate its owner's power and influence. This makes perfect business sense but has no humanitarian sense.

It should be clear to everyone that the money system does not even attempt to address the issues of people; it holds us back, creates its own twisted logic and empowers this tiny elite and actually guarantees war. That's right – money guarantees war. The majority of people in society do not want or seek war, but it always seems to happen; this should be a clear indication that government does not reflect the will of those it should serve and is following its own agenda. There is a reason for this which becomes apparent when the effect of war is thought about. Government in a money economy does not serve the needs of people and war is actually very attractive. It allows a nation to acquire the resources of another in order to enrich itself and allows the aggressor nation to prop up its political and social systems, maintaining the status quo, rather than effectively dealing with its issues. Think of a man too lazy to cultivate his garden; he waits for his neighbours land to be fruitful then takes it – this is essentially what war is.

An excellent example of this is the fact that the US consumes more than 25 per cent of the world's oil yet it produces around 3 per cent. This is obviously an unsustainable situation and a serious problem in a money system and war becomes inevitable. Rather than address the real issue of quickly reducing oil consumption to sustainable levels (which is a very expensive research and development process with no immediate benefit by way of profit) it is cheaper and more profitable to just take the resources of another nation and install a leader there who is responsive to the needs of the aggressor nation. Another problem with addressing the real issue under a money system is; who is willing and can pay for doing the right thing?

It is simply more profitable to kill, destroy and maim than it is to re-think and restructure the energy needs of the aggressor nation peacefully. It remains the principal of slave and slave master played out on an international stage; it remains the lazy, but aggressive neighbour. Another clear benefit of war to the establishment is that each missile, each tank, plane, gun and bullet, body armour and body bag represents an item of profit for a corporation somewhere. While people are dying and civilian lives disrupted there is an elite group of people growing fat from the financial profits of suffering. They are remote and distant from the smell of death, living fantastic lifestyles whilst the profits they make buy respect that they don't deserve and acceptance when they should be vilified and exposed as the inhuman beasts they are. But of course these people can buy us and are even seen as role-models of success, so we try to please them for an opportunity to earn some of their money.

Additionally, war provides profit because of the cost of rebuilding the vanquished nation. With so many benefits of war it is easy to see why we are told things to scare us about the 'enemy' and have us demand wars that we don't want to fight. In our current society, war has been the major driver for techno-logical advancement and people have benefited from its ancillary and 'spin-off' developments. The prospect of dropping bombs on the heads of people drove the development of flight and later came pleasure flights for us. The need to maintain military communications in the event of nuclear attack spawned the internet. Imagine if we actually intended to help people when we put work into technology.

It does not reflect our wishes that developing the first nuclear bomb cost the equivalent of 24 Billion of 2008 US dollars and employed 130,000 highly skilled workers.[28] It does not reflect our wishes that the Strategic Defence Initiative beloved of President Reagan cost in excess of US$100 Billion. Or the recent

Emergency Economic Stabilisation Act of 2008, signed by President Bush cost in excess of US$700 Billion in America alone (which allowed the banking institutions to continue to pay themselves generous personal bonuses). Again we see the old Egyptian principal of huge resources taken from many to benefit the few. We could have cured cancer with that level of commitment or housed and fed every human and addressed a galaxy of human distress. But the elite's priorities are different from ours and their spending priorities reflect it.

Money maintains the social hierarchy and reduces the ability of normal people to oppose the things done in our name with our taxes. The existence of money allows those few that control it to make decisions, regardless how unpopular, with virtually no effective opposition. Even those of us that live in countries with democratic pretensions still find ourselves unable to affect the direction that our government set for us. We live under the tyranny of the ballot box. We elect a leader based upon his promises, then find ourselves unable to influence any decision made once that individual is in office; promises kept or not. Our only recourse is to use our vote differently at the next elections and keep the circle of political abuse going.

Even when inhumane decisions are made, those individuals motivated and brave enough to protest find themselves facing the might of the nation's police and find their views distorted by the media. The irony is that the taxes the protesters are paying contribute to the cruelty they are trying to stop. In fact, under a money economy taxes are a prerequisite for governments to gather the resources and soldiers they need to take us into war. It is us who pay for these wars of acquisition, it is us that fight, are mutilated, die for those acquisitions (then struggle to meet our basic human needs), yet it is the corporations and governments that collect the profit. It is because of our engineered dependence on money that we compromise our basic good nature and accept a role killing people we don't know – it is because we need cash to feed ourselves that we build the bombs that kill people that have not harmed us or our family. Because of our need for money we accept the terrible things that happen around us; in fact, the dependence on money causes people to feel helpless, stop thinking and close down their humanity.

For example, on TV you have no doubt seen advertisements urging you to send a few pounds or dollars to a worthy charity. But, you worked hard for the money and you need it for your own needs and you cannot be certain the money you send ends up where it is needed anyway, so the TV channel is changed and you watch something that distracts you instead.[29] The good causes continue to struggle and although we have enough compared to the suffering we see, we are conditioned into thinking we have nothing to give or not enough saved and that we are powerless to affect change.

That distracting influence helps us reconcile ourselves to the status quo, promotes our sense of helplessness and is another prop to the money system and its elite. The media and the information we are provided with goes through a filtering process very similar to that of new ideas. We are told a filtered truth that may take into account the views and direction of the people that pay the wages. We don't get informed of the harmful ingredients in our food, the real reason for protest, or of the true story before a country is invaded in our name by our husbands, sons and fathers and increasingly, wives, partners, daughters and mothers. There are a number of public interest stories that have either been suppressed or watered down or even exaggerated because of vested interest, with the only way for us to know the activities of our Representatives being through unofficially leaked information. Without the fear of Weapons of Mass Destruction (ready to strike within 45 minutes) would we have supported our government in invading Iraq? Is there any relevance to the fact that the American Television News channel NBC is owned by General Electric? (GE is a major defence contractor to the government of the United States of America and there are other connections between the media and defence contractors.)[30] Do we have reason to totally trust the motivations of our media?

A clear and constant dilemma that a media editor faces is whether to publish a story that might impact on the advertising revenues and therefore the profits of the operation. The editor knows that his family's financial security is at risk if he chooses to publish or broadcast the whole truth if it is against the interests of his patrons. His performance is measured by the financial success of the organisation rather than the quality of journalism. Of course the support of advertisers is key to this success and the threat of a large account withdrawing their patronage is a potent tool in ensuring compliance with the official story that the public sees. The editor has the additional problem of knowing that any independent action could result in him being unable to ever achieve another position of equivalent income and status again.

A good example among many is Steve Wilson and Jane Akre, television journalists who were making a documentary about Posilac and its dangers for Fox Television in America. When the journalists refused to compromise the content of their broadcast, they were dismissed by their employers after pressure from Posilac's makers, Monsanto Corporation. They were 'fired' for doing their job correctly but contradicting the needs of a small powerful group. It is reported in June 1998 that a Fox official said 'we paid $3 billion for these stations. We'll decide what the news is'[31]. The journalists work was clearly in the best interests of the world's population to know that we are potentially being poisoned but under a money system a rich few always outweigh the needs of the rest of us.

Wilson and Akre showed a great deal of integrity but that kind of personal pressure is almost impossible to withstand and it is easy to see how the information we rely on can easily be tainted. These scenarios are played out against a back-drop of it not being legally necessary to broadcast or publish unbiased truth in many countries.[32] The impact of this is profound. The owners of the media have enormous power to express their views and suppress the publishing of any inconvenient information. This also encourages the news providers to filter the news to form and lead public opinion in accordance with the media owners wishes. Instead of clear, unbiased, balanced and fair reporting of facts, we have media that tells us what to think and how to react. In England we have had tabloid newspapers claim responsibility for election results[33] and/or threatening political leaders with a campaign of editorialising against them. Often the media conducts staged ideological arguments within itself that only divide people and distract us from the real issues. The real issue is that politics conducted against a backdrop of a money economy is entirely illusionary, a little bit crazy and humans are suffering.

The situation becomes sinister if the media owner happens to have financial interest in other activities that a journalist may otherwise be interested in or media interests that cross national borders, i.e. if a newspaper owner has a financial interest in a drug company; are we likely to have full and critical reporting in the event of a problem there?

It is the media that directs our attention away from the things important to human lives and towards the pressing issue of a celebrity's haircut. It is in the interests of mainstream media to support the status quo whether it works for us or not, because it's first priority is self interest and quick profit. It is the media that ensures that we keep the creaking, failing money system going; they present us with the odd story of the lottery winner or the exceptional individual who beats the odds and becomes successful in this rigged game. It is the exceptional nature of the story that makes it news worthy but it has the effect of keeping us hopeful but simultaneously robbing us of our pride and self-esteem, because we cannot be successful when others clearly can.

We feel powerless to manage our own lives let alone change the awful things that are occurring around the world, so we switch off our minds to the problems and embrace the distractions.

But, even the distractions we are presented with show the distorted priorities of our current system. A popular entertainer or successful sportsperson can be rewarded with more money in a month than someone offering an essential service, such as a fire-fighter who regularly risks their life, will earn in more than 15 years of service to the community. Whose priority does this represent? Certainly not ours! Is it that an entertainer helps maintain and enforce our status quo by keeping us distracted?

Religion

Established religion also has a part to play. This book is not intended to cause offence or to express disrespect for the heartfelt views that people may hold. This book is intended to encourage dispassionate thought about the impact that religion has on their lives and to think independently of conditioning.

Religion has offered great comfort to individuals as they have struggled to reconcile the hardships of their lives. It has given meaning and order to a society that makes no sense, but has allowed the establishment to mould society with less inter-ference.

Often, however, religion has done more than just observe the impact of unequal distribution of resources and encourage its followers to accept their lowly status. Religion was once described as "the opium of the people" because it encourages a submissive attitude and submission to hierarchies. But, it too, as an institution, has sought to ensure its own survival by any means necessary, and has swayed under pressure, endorsing or leaving unchallenged some of the questionable things prominent individuals, corporations or governments have done. It has historically supported the establishment rather than insist that each human has a life of dignity and emotional self development.

There have been many historical events where churches have supported wars of acquisition in God's name and endorsed regimes we would consider to be repugnant. There has been many examples of Holy War were one church chooses to prove its closer connection to God through destroying a competitor religion or nation in combat and acquiring their resources and followers. In Iraq now there are evangelical Southern Baptist missionaries[34] who distribute food parcels in public, but whose internal documents stress the religious conversions of Muslims to Christianity and their intent to 'save souls'. At such a contentious time these activities are, at the very least insensitive if not disrespectful and it is certain that these missionaries would be very unwelcoming if roles were reversed. The tendency of one faith to disparage the views of others is further illustrated by the fact that (at the time of writing), an arms supplier to the US Army, Trijicom Corporation stamps bible verses on the weapons used by American troops.

Furthermore, there are many faiths that require their numbers to prove Godliness by how much money they give or the converts they make. And many religious organisations define themselves by their secular power, litigiousness and influence.

I have recently heard it said by US vice Presidential candidate Sarah Palin that the Iraq war was God's will. I sincerely doubt God has an interest in which fraction of humanity secures the commercial rights to resources that should be available to us all. Neither is He likely to approve of the millions murdered, injured, made homeless and suffering for oil, when we are capable of simply bypassing this dependency.

Religion in its current form is a drag on human progress because it asks its members to accept many things without recourse to individual thought and distracts us from the overwhelming similarities of people, stopping us addressing problems. It is one of the tools of Empire, dividing us into xenophobic, warring groups and encouraging us to accept orders from our group leaders without question . It gives another reason for one man to fear and distrust another and acts as a cheerleader to the questionable actions our governments choose to take, often remaining inappropriately silent in the face of state-sponsored crime.

Established religion holds amazing wealth. What does it do with it? Any established religion could end world hunger. Even the poorest countries lavish money on religious buildings and structures whilst people literally outside these structures can starve.

I am sure you see by now the theme of divide and conquer that the money economy actually guarantees and that religion, with its rules of conditioned submission and hereafter punishments, encourages. We need to adjust the nature of religion; we need to replace dogma and reject our inability to recognise the humanity of someone who is different and not be afraid of them because they are not in our particular club.

We need to replace religious dogma with our own creed. I would suggest 'only do good by all'. If established religion/society/people would accept these simple words, soldiers would put down their guns, arms makers would find the production rooms empty of staff, Government would be forced by us to address problems in a sensible and mature manner and leaders could no longer drag us into never-ending wars.

All of us can still worship our own God in whatever form that takes and not impose our religious views on others or take political decisions from a dogmatic pre-supposition. But before this can happen we need to recognise our strength and importance because nothing happens without us to do it. We also need to reject our current status as a resource to be used then discarded; we need to recognise more of our human similarities than our differences.

4

Why Money Based Economies Cause Unnecessary Hunger, Starvation & Other Resource Shortages

The world is very different now. For man holds in his mortal hands the power to abolish all forms of human poverty, and all forms of human life.

John F Kennedy

At some stage most people have wondered why starvation and hunger exists. We have all been haunted by the image of the child with his stomach distended, too exhausted to clear the insects from his face. Yet there never seems to be enough political will to deal with this basic problem and so it continues.

Many point to the countries that have successfully used the monetary system to substantially deal with widespread famine, hunger and starvation; which such countries as China, Russia and India have fairly recently dealt with and which virtually all nations have experienced at some time.

Many people think of hunger as being caused by an absolute shortage of food and it is therefore inevitable that some humans will experience hunger or slow starvation. This, however, has long been known not to be the case. Adam Smith the pioneer of modern economic philosophy in his book *The Wealth of Nations* published in 1776 set out the thinking that has influenced most national and international economic thinking ever since, particularly in capitalist nations.

In simple terms he theorised that self interested resource suppliers would always provide the needs of those that demand a service or resource and the market would always reach equilibrium i.e., supply would always match demand if a market was left alone to operate. He did however caveat that monopoly supplier situations must be avoided. In practical terms this means that if the people of a nation were experiencing food shortage, the price would increase and more suppliers would be encouraged into meeting the need. Therefore if the price is attractive enough ordinary members of the public would devote their private gardens to supply a food demand. Therefore should a nation experience a harvest shortfall, it simply uses its *entitlement* (money) to meet its needs by paying for food from anyone that has it, wherever they are and with all possible speed.Therefore the ability to pay represents entitlement to be fed.

Money creates a demand for goods and services and NOT the people that need them. Money exclusively represents the needs of people.

According to Adam Smith's theory a nation that suffers widespread hunger and starvation simply does not have the *entitlement* to have their human needs satisfied unless they can pay. No purchasing power represents no entitlement and therefore no trigger for needed action, so in a market/money based economy there has simply been nothing for the market to respond to. People can die because of a lack of purchasing power rather than a shortage of food itself. This is why we have virtually constant appeals from charity, because our donations are used to create an *economic entitlement*. The hungry are therefore an overhead that people, nations and the current economic system simply ignores because helping the starving impacts on the money of those helping, rather than resource availability being limited.

Amartya Kumar Sen winner of the 1998 Nobel Memorial Prize in Economic Sciences, lived through the famine in Bengal in 1943 and later studied the economics of that event. Fundamentally, he found that India indeed had the food resources to deal with the issue without outside help, but the sufferers had insufficient money to exercise their entitlement to food once prices increased. Food producers in other parts of India could not afford to simply give their surpluses away and the transportation system could not afford to give its carrying capacity for nothing, as a result approximately three millions died entirely unnecessarily.

This is in brief terms the economic anatomy of hunger and starvation but the issue does not end in the vulnerable third world. In the world's richest nation there are serious ongoing issues around food that no-one appears able to address.

The Food Research and Action Centre (FRAC) is a non profit organisation devoted to eradicating hunger and under-nutrition within America itself. It reports that in 2008, 49.1 million people, including 16.7 million children live in households that suffer hunger and/or experience food insecurity. It also reports that shortly half of all American children are expected to be requiring government support in meeting their nutritional needs. This is the same nation that the Centers of Disease Control and Prevention reports that in 2008, at least 20% of their entire population is medically obese and this figure is trending upwards.

There is surely no food shortage in America, there is simply an inability of a sizeable and growing number of people to exercise their entitlement to food and those that have the power to change the situation simply chose not to, whether the sufferers are starving in the third world or going hungry in America.

The issue is not that food is in short supply. The solution to the world's food, water and environmental needs can quite easily be resolved once the profit motive is removed from human problem solving. It merely requires that the relevant engineers /designers come together and develop the best processes available within the resources available and for technicians to implement it and distribute the results in the most effective manner for addressing human need.

The existence of people on our earth inevitably causes an impact as we make changes to improve our standard of living. We currently use money to decide how we manage our environment and it is the needs of money that currently have priority over the needs of the planet, people animals and flora. Removing money as a consideration allows us to concentrate purely on the outcomes we seek; sustainable improvements in the quality of all our lives. For example, this approach would allow people to replace every vehicle with a green alternative very quickly, thus slashing emissions at a stroke. We could do this right now but it will not happen because of the issue of who will pay.

The solution to food concerns can also be addressed with innovative methods for expanding supply. New approaches to supply issues are again hamstrung by the imperative to make immediate financial sense. Yet there are many practical options open to us, i.e., allocating more land to food production by converting unused dessert land which cannot be affected by GM or other contaminants. Or if that is considered ineffective, virtually every country today has underground tunnels (in cities, through mountains and under seas) mainly used for transportation. We could create caverns or tunnels and equip them with sunlight replication systems, crop appropriate climate management and optimised organic soil in order to expand the crop-baring capacity of our planet and ensure that every harvest is an optimal harvest. The roofs of our sky-scrapers can also be used for hydroponics production. We could use innovations like these and others to free up space for the humane and natural rearing of more livestock and develop sustainable and effective methods of transport to ensure food is where it is needed.

Everything people have made or created either came from the earth, her plant life or animals, but without human ingenuity there would have been no progress and no possibility of achieving a modern lifestyle. The items key to human life today are plastics, metals, fabrics, building materials, wood, chemicals and of course energy. Our primary concerns should be the effective use of, and effective re-cycling of materials. According to 'Vital Waste Graphics 2. The Basel Conversation' the average person in the prosperous west creates between 45 and 85 tonnes of waste material each year, which is unsustainable but clearly addressable. More effective use of available resources enables more people to have their human needs met whilst minimising our impact on the earth. But, until money is removed as the main influence behind our decisions, change will not come. Our current economy is clearly no longer fit for purpose.

5

Our Current Political Options & How Money Controls All

A house divided against itself cannot stand

Abraham Lincoln

We can see that the purpose of any economy should be to use the earth's resources to satisfy human need and we have seen how a money economy perverts that. Now it is appropriate to examine the social science of politics.

Politics is the process by which people make collective, group, national or international decisions. There is usually an element of delegation of authority and powers of regulation over the group. Group decision making (politics) and the use of the earth's resources (economics) are irrevocably tied together, because group decisions always relate to the acquisition, management, creation and distribution of needed resources. Humans have over time had leaderships and decision making based on one of two basic principals:

Authoritarianism

This is the obvious rule of the few taking the form of Absolute Monarchies and other dictatorships etc. There are other variations of authoritarian rule which won't be discussed here, but they all hold in common;

- Distain for the rights and needs of individuals outside of the ruling group.
- Strict control over available resources and their distribution.

- Often there is a system of rewards and punishments aimed at protecting the leadership.
- A despotic outcome with cruelty inherent in the way resources are distributed to the group.
- The leadership encourage loyalty to themselves at the expense of all other priorities as a means of maintaining power. This can be achieved by the adoption of state religions, popular entertainments as distractions and strong police or military forces to control dissent.
- The group are encouraged to be concerned for themselves only and not their neighbour. There may be encouragement to disrespect people unless they are the same religion, culture or ethnicity. The divide and rule principal.
- Minimal ability for the group or population to affect decisions, be represented or influence how resources are distributed. There is secrecy around key decisions that affect the group and biased information provided to them.
- Reduced ability for group individuals to determine the circumstances of their own lives. There are major disparities between rich and poor; the poorest experiencing severe hardship with restricted ability to make changes without the support/involvement of the ruling clique.
- There is often a fear of outsiders encouraged to reduce external influences, with movements of individuals restricted in and out of the nation.

In summary, they are the governments where available resources are retained to satisfy the wants of the ruling class, whilst ignoring the needs of the general population. There is inherent cruelty yet those suffering are unable to affectively admonish or influence those in authority. This is the kind of government ran by the Egyptians, Germany under the Nazi's, seen today in North Korea and other nations. They are despised regimes, often characterised by the lengths their population will go to in attempting to leave. There is therefore an inherent weakness or lack of stability to those regimes because eventually the citizens "wake up" and take action to free themselves from their abusive treatment. History is full of revolts and bloody revolutions that happen as a result of inequitable distribution of resources.

Democracy – The Rule of the Many

In it's ideal form democracy is where a population makes the key decisions about how resources are to be sourced, produced and distributed amongst itself. In it's ideal form the population determine how they live their lives and the behaviour expectations of individuals inside the group.

At our current stage of development, the world's leading democracies practice something called Parliamentary or Representative government. This is where the population elect individuals to represent them and act in the electorate's best interest. However, these elected politicians are not limited in their powers and therefore hold enough authority to act under their own initiative. This also means these elected representatives have the authority within their position to act according to their own wishes even if this contradicts the promises made whilst campaigning for office and the intent of the electorate that put them in place. This is clearly a hugely contentious point that needs clear examples to justify this stance and the world's most powerful 'democracy' America has many clear examples of the weaknesses of the Representative or Parliamentary method.

The people of the world's richest and militarily most powerful nation regularly fund wars conducted on foreign soil yet cannot find a way of addressing their own health needs. America currently has a health system based on each individual paying an insurance premium to a privately owned business that subsequently pays the hospitals or other care providers when/if treatment is needed.

The system has several serious but predictable problems.

The first being that around 15.4% or 46.3 million[35] people in America cannot afford insurance, consequently 44,000 American's die each year from preventable conditions. There is a site that records many of their sad stories.[36] Second, a study found[37] in 2007, 62% of all bankruptcies were linked to medical expenses.

Third, the insurance industry has steadily increased profits by increasing health insurance premiums which have increased by more than 130% over the last decade for family coverage, far outstripping inflation. Yet, the insurance industry sets limits on the expense that a sick person can incur, regardless of need.

Forth, the health insurance industry has taken to cancelling insurance policies because of pre-existing conditions and small print violations whilst employees are paid to find ways of declining unprofitable clients. The US Government House Subcommittee on Oversight and Investigations found in June 2009 that three medical insurance companies had between them cancelled more than 20,000 people/policies to avoid making payouts after accepting payments.[38] Policies cancelled include babies with no other issues than being considered too large or too small to be profitable,[39] the victims of domestic abuse and those with family health issues.

Fifth, in America many employers offer health insurance benefits in lieu of higher salary opportunities. This leaves the employee very dependent on their employer and facing serious difficulties if that employer chooses to reduce the cover or goes out of business.

Naturally, Americans themselves find this situation unsatisfactory and according to a 2009 poll by New York Times/CBS News, 85% said the healthcare system had to be fundamentally changed or entirely rebuilt. President Obama was elected on a campaign of "Change You Can Believe In", yet despite overwhelming support from his electors, Obama appears unable to deliver what he promised and what his electors need.

The reason is simple and again obvious under a Representative Democratic system combined with a money based system. The insurance industry is an exceptionally powerful lobbying force. It spends on average US$1.4m per day to persuade our representatives not to allow any significant change[40] and 2009 persuading our representatives is expected to exceed US$500m. The brazen-ness is stunning. The industry collect's peoples' money for an essential service, it maximises profit at the expense of the lives of their customers, then uses that profit to stop their clients from achieving a better deal.

The failing nature of the Representative Democratic process is further illustrated by the fact that the Senator in charge of drafting the new legislation is the single largest recipient of insurance industry funds, whilst his advisers have financial interest in the current system and are therefore unwilling to meet the needs of the electorate they should be serving.

In the world's most powerful democracy our representatives mostly depend on funds from corporations to finance their attempts to gain political office. The more money they receive, the more media airtime they can buy to promote themselves. However, the relationship between our representatives and the corporations does not end at direct campaign contributions. A good example of this is Bristol Palin, the 19 year old daughter of US Vice Presidential candidate Sarah Palin. Bristol enterprisingly started her own Public Relations firm BSMP LLC to promote conservative Pro Abstinence Sex Education Programmes. Apparently BSMP LLC has several lucrative accounts and attracts generous donations from corporations. There are few 19 year olds that would attract that kind of support. The reason those businesses choose to support Bristol Palin is likely because they may be investing in the future success of Sarah, her mother and hoping to generate goodwill.

But the Palin family is one of many political families that benefit in this and other similar ways. Another benefit that our representatives receive is the lucrative jobs awaiting those leaving office. For example, ex Prime Minister Tony Blair commands at least £100,000 for each 90 minute speech. Bill Clinton in 2005 earned US$7.5m from giving speeches upon retirement,[41] generous book deals and appearance fees from corporations reward the accommodating politician. There are numerous examples where our representatives await their reward for services rendered with honorarium positions and other benefits that could compromise their ability to represent the electorate without prejudice.

The affect of all this is the representative becomes more important and powerful than the represented, than the group from which they come and "we the people" can do little to change things even if we demand it and vote for it constitutionally.

The sad thing is that the current system encourages dishonesty and deception towards us the represented, as the politicians protect their privileged positions. Again the healthcare debate in the US is a great example. Rather than debate the issue in a sensible manner that addresses human need, we have representatives inventing scare stories about "death panels"; where sick people are expected to plead for their lives before a bureaucrat. Other politicians speak in terms of health care reform as a Communist take over, fear the cost of change (cost doesn't matter where war is concerned), express concern that floods of foreigners will swamp the new care system or doctors will be forced to compromise their Hippocratic oath.

Rather than deal with the issues in a manner that the electorate want, our representatives confuse and complicate what is essentially a simple directive. Our current democracy is failing the people. In fact our democracy is clearly mutating into a corpocracy.

Corpocracy is a form of government better suited to the Authoritarian or rule by the few bracket described earlier. In this case however, major business is the ruling clique, using their financial strength to influence politicians and control the state.

Again, this is an important observation and requires examples that we all experience to back it up. The Credit Crunch is an excellent illustration of why we no longer live in a functioning democracy but now suffer under authoritarian rule.

We're not going to rehearse the causes etc here, there are other books that study the mechanics of the problem. We'll be briefly looking at the attitudes of government, the solutions they propose to ease the distress of their electorates and what they intend to prevent it happening again and whether it can be achieved.

When the first American banks were unable to meet their contractual payments to creditors, the financial system went into panic. Creditors worldwide ceased further lending in order to audit and understand the potential loses faced. This cessation of lending had catastrophic effect on business, the property markets and the people that depended on credit in order to make a living. Businesses and individuals dependent on the availability of credit found themselves unable to trade and bankruptcies, insolvencies, hunger and homelessness numbers jumped hugely overnight in the prosperous countries. The world's most feared nation found tent cities emerging in the warmer states, where the repossessed and newly homeless were placed by the authorities.[42]

Our representatives reacted to the crisis by borrowing money (which we repay) and creating valueless money for the benefit of keeping the banks in business, effectively making bank profit private but socialising bank loses. Meanwhile reporters like Rick Santelli on CNBC News (on location at the trading centre of

Chicago) animatedly rails against helping the 'losers' with their mortgages and calls for further 'reward [for] people who can carry the water instead of drink the water'. Santelli is literally applauded by the financial industry people that cause the problems. Other reporters also of CNBC News launch a fierce defence of why the banking institutions still deserve their large personal bonuses, despite the devastation in the real economy and the fact the taxpayer is now suffering serious consequences.[43] Yet the Governor of South Carolina (Mark Sanford) offered unemployed people his prayers whilst refusing to distribute funds intended to help the people he represented.[44] In England, John Healy, Housing Minister in a left of centre government is on record as saying that losing your home through repossession can be a good thing. This from a man meant to represent us and who made significant personal profit because of taxpayer subsidised housing.[45] Maybe it could be argued that Sanford or Healy was presenting the views of the majority of his constituents when he refused help for the suffering, however it is unlikely that these constituents would agree to being lied to under any circumstances. But this happens all the time in a Representative Democracy.

At a time like this, it is natural that our governments, the general business community and people are anxious to ensure another *credit crunch* can never happen again and to that end there are many financial experts working on reforming the system. Reform of the current system is clearly an essential priority with the electorate needing to protect their homes, pensions, livelihoods and security. Governments need it to create a stable financial environment to please the electorate and affirm their political positions. Yet, because we want it and we are the overwhelming majority, it is not guaranteed that we'll get it.

Prominent American political consultant, Frank Luntz had advised on how to successfully delay and frustrate the national demand for healthcare change. Another memo penned by Frank

Luntz was leaked early 2010 which contained detailed instructions on how to oppose financial reform whilst giving voters the impression that they are acting in the best interests of the population and not special money interests.[46]

Our system is failing us because it encourages dishonesty in our leadership, it keeps the population away from key decisions, encourages a dishonest presentation of the facts and therefore fails to work in our best interests.

There were eleven key distinguishing features of totalitarian government in the previous section of the book. If you review those features you'll find that all but two apply to our great western democracies.

Our current political process is clearly not fit for purpose.

6

Impact of Money on Individuals

I do not deny that many appear to have succeeded in a material way by cutting corners and by manipulating associates.

Alan Greenspan

Money has an impact on almost every human decision; it impacts on marriage and divorce; it creates and destroys friendships and families; those that are wealthy become more attractive for their money rather than their personal qualities. There was a comedienne interviewing an attractive young lady married to a much older and certainly less attractive man, she started the conversation with 'what was it that first attracted you to the multimillionaire…?' It impacts on how we live, how we use our recreation time and the tasks we accept; it even causes us to accept actions in ourselves and others that would make no sense otherwise. Here is an example of how money overwhelms your better nature:

Imagine two criminals come to your home; you are totally safe from violence or reprisals in any way and the authorities do not know and never will that these people came to your home. At your home there are no children and no threat to property. Both criminals ask to spend the night on your living room floor; one criminal offers you a life-changing amount of money ($/£1m) and the other offers you nothing. Knowing yourself to be safe – what do you do? Ask among your friends and colleagues and you'll find that nine out of ten would accept the cash, even though they are doing the wrong thing.

Another example:

> When you are financially under pressure and concerned about
> fuelling your car or paying utility bills – do you still give to
> the homeless guy any reasonable amount of money. Again at
> least eight out of ten will answer negatively, consoling
> themselves with the belief/thought that the homeless guy will
> only use our money for drugs or alcohol and we're certain he
> contributed to his problems.

It is hard to be a generous human being in a monetary society,
because helping someone often means making yourself more
financially vulnerable. Recent joint experiments between the
universities of Minnesota and Florida State found that personal
relationships and interpersonal sensitivity declined where
money is involved.

The problems caused by money come closer to home than the
way we deal with casual or professional contacts. Animal
charities report that during periods of economic recession the
number of previously loved pets that are abandoned or left
without medical treatment skyrockets.[47] The emotional trauma
experienced by that family as they examine and re-examine their
budget must be heart rendering, to force them to act so cruelly,
but what is their choice?

Money forces good people to live their lives from a place of
fear and imagined scarcity. The fear of scarcity causes people to
compromise their good nature in order to secure their own
survival. People then form political groupings and ultimately
methods of governance that reflect the individual's perceived
relationship with, and access to money – left wing and right wing
(of the political spectrum) opposing the other, wasting resources,
time and energy disagreeing over the distribution, availability
and use of money completely missing the point that resources
and goods are important not illusionary money. Whilst those that

control this commodity and can actually address human issues are not held to account.

Again, it is a matter of record that during recessionary times, extreme political parties experience rapid recruitment growth; hate speech and scape-goating of minority groups becomes more prevalent,[48] with people seeking to place blame rather than actually deal with the problem head-on. During recessionary times the shortage of money causes an increase in domestic violence, relationship pressures and increases in violent crime with robbery as a motive,[49/2] whilst the social elite are entirely untouched by our difficulties. They have priority access to the commodity we all need and control of the money available to the rest of us.

Money has an established link to crime. I'm not excusing criminal behaviour (personal responsibility for our actions is one key to the solution) but the lack of cash and the fear of a lack of cash is an accepted cause for criminality causing a percentage of people to override their inclination towards good in the fight to find the resources to feed, clothe and house themselves and their dependents.

The inequalities of the money system are admitted by many Governments that offer varying levels of welfare benefits. But even welfare programmes fail in achieving their intended goal, by creating dependencies and twisting some recipient's talents into exploiting the system. It has been noted that people who are receiving social benefits quite often have more children than other socio-economic groups. A contributor to this trend is the fact that each child represents further state support by way of housing and cash. This trend is also seen in third world countries where individuals have as many children as they can, first to compensate for high infant mortality rates and secondly to replace a money pension in their old age. These children can often be forced into work to create an income for the parents or daughters sold into the sex industry. It is no coincidence that wealthier people tend to have fewer children than the poor[50] – they already are secure.

Because our system inevitably generates winners and losers; even in the best economic times there are unemployed people that must observe the apparent prosperity of those around them. The world's wealthiest nations still have citizens suffering homelessness and hunger and it is all unnecessary. In America as many as 3,000,000 people are homeless in any given year;[51] in Europe the number is similar 'despite the fact that Europe considers itself more socially responsible than America'.[52] The futility of it all is apparent when you are aware that vacant properties would house all of these people. But the homeless cannot pay for those empty homes and it makes financial sense to leave the homeless in the cold and the properties empty.

We have situations in the UK where children can be separated from their parents when the family home is repossessed. In the United Kingdom people who are unable to meet their mortgage payments are considered to have made themselves intentionally homeless and ineligible for state assistance. However, Social Services have an obligation to ensure that young children are not exposed to a life on the streets. Increasingly cash strapped government agencies are being forced to place children in foster family care, whilst the natural parents can be left to fend for themselves or to depend on charities like Save The Family.

Even those that fit into the system, earn a respectable living and enjoy some status are suffering under the system. They often work at tasks they don't enjoy or work long hours putting relationships with partners and children under strain. As mentioned earlier statistically the majority of these will still struggle to achieve security through their savings and there is a clear economic reason for this that the social elite benefit from.

Over the past decades cheap technology has been introduced to the workplace which has dramatically increased worker output/productivity and this allows businesses to achieve great production increases whilst making employees redundant. This improvement in productivity now allows business to reduce the cost of their goods and services to the consumer, which is great. However, this improvement also means the pool of under-employed labour increases and the influence of the unions dramatically curtailed and employees are therefore unable to achieve pay rises that are equitable to the increased work they must now do. The failure of pay rises to keep up with increased production is actually a transfer of wealth from employee to employer. This is why the rich get richer whilst everyone else struggles.

Whenever an employer makes a position redundant, yet asks the remaining staff to cover that workload without significant extra pay, wealth is being transferred from the employee to the corporation. When production goes up yet pay rises are tied to inflation or foregone because of unpredictable economic times, wealth is being transferred from the employee to the corporation – no wonder people cannot save; their savings are going to the corporation. But the employee is rarely in the position to resist the swindle because there is always a dozen people behind them coveting their job.

This is why people never seem to get ahead even though they work very hard to create financial security for themselves. This also explains why the gap between boardroom and shop floor pay has widened with the richest British being 100 times better off than their poorer neighbours.[53] Yet, it is logical that the boardroom will continue to seek further efficiencies regardless of the wider negative effects.

But even those few fortunate enough to have the work/life balance just right and that have achieved financial security face the issues of protecting themselves and family from jealous, dangerous people. In the USA they may choose to live in gated and security guarded communities.[54] They must protect themselves from people that seek to abuse their friendships by asking for money. They have to take precautions to protect their wealth from predatory divorces and gold-diggers, and oppose measures that seek to redistribute and erode the difference between them and the majority of the people they see. As this individual becomes conspicuous in their wealth, they lose their freedom to walk the public street without physical risk or unreasonable intrusion into their privacy by others seeking to make a living selling photographs or gossip; their children become a target for kidnap and ransom demands. This individual quickly learns to distrust those around them, often culminating in emotional issues, loneliness or perceived comfort in narcotics; these are embattled and stressed people.[55] The wealth of certain individuals can even distort genuine friendships and change the personality of the newly wealthy, into someone who cannot be certain his friends are genuinely interested in him.[56]

But consider the following scenario which would have unfolded in prosperous Iceland but for the intervention of several Governments and international agencies:

The day the Iceland Banks found they were unable to meet their loan repayment commitments their cash holdings with institutions outside of Iceland would be frozen. In order to prevent depositors demanding the return of their savings and investments the banks would close themselves to both accepting and releasing cash. A local wealthy Icelandic account holder would find that his credit card would be declined at the food store and his debit card is refused too because his bank is insolvent. A trip to his bank finds the doors closed and a large unhappy crowd outside it. He finds that the shops and petrol/gas stations will only accept cash and he finds the cash he carries in his pocket doesn't go far.

Over the next few days he notices that payments due to him have no way of reaching him, nor can he make the payments to others that he should. He also notices the shops are slow to replenish their stock and prices rise sharply. It turns out the bank collapse took the funds belonging to the shops and businesses too, so workers go unpaid and only a few continue with their duties. Only a few shops are able to pay their suppliers and prices go up further to pay for the armed guards needed to protect the buildings from hungry violent crowds. It is not long before he is unsuccessfully trying to sell jewellery and other luxury items for food and to keep the power on in his wonderful home as the crowds become more and more desperate and government struggles to maintain order with unpaid police. Our Icelandic millionaire is now afraid of violence from people he is unable to pay and people who perceive him to still be wealthy.

But the strangest thing is that there is no change in the food available to them and no change in the world's resources; the crops in the fields are still growing, the cows are still producing milk, yet society crumbles. The line between civilisation and chaos will always be this fine and insecure under a money system. But even with external financial support, Iceland has indeed experienced riots and civil disorder caused by their problems with an illusionary commodity.

7

The Role of Technology in a Monetary Society

At least I don't have to deal with the robots union.

Henry Ford

We've already touched on the fact that ordinary people most often benefit from technology in a 'trickle down' manner. For example, we benefit from non-stick cookware as a result of the efforts put into space exploration. Our access to wireless communications and the air safety benefits of radar are as a result of developing more efficient ways of conducting war. The inventions solely intended for human benefit (domestic appliances, etc) have mainly come from individuals who then have to pass through the filtering process already described, often spending years trying to persuade the establishment of their products merit and, more often than not, failing to find anyone with the financial ability to sponsor it.

It is clear then that technology is not often developed with us directly in mind and technological improvement is mostly driven by the war machine and corporations whose first priority is, of course, to their own continued financial prosperity. Because this kind of research and development is mostly funded by corporations, it is no surprise to discover that new technology often takes the form of equipment or machinery that is not directly relevant to our lives.

The vehicle manufacturing industry is a good example here. The moving assembly line was introduced by Henry Ford around 1908 and this concept made the motor car cheap enough to be accessible to more than the super rich, until then the car was made by highly skilled craftsmen for a limited client base. The manufacturing process was still labour intensive but the strenuous and unrelenting pressure of the job, with each discrete task closely timed meant that Ford workers earned every penny of their relatively well-paid, but stressful and dehumanising employment. Vehicle building was a major driver of economic prosperity in America and other Western nations; it also marked improvement in the standard of living for those that could afford this new technology. The success (in terms of reducing the cost of car making) of the moving assembly line forced European manufacturers to adopt the revolutionary process pioneered by Henry Ford or face bankruptcy. Citroen in France was the first to succumb to the pressure to be more efficient; the rest soon followed. The pressure to constantly improve financial efficiency in a monetary system, forces this industry (a major employer) and all other industries to design systems, technologies and processes that replace people with machines and reduce their costs regardless of the impact on staff. Therefore, there are wave after wave of redundancies, each time a manufacturing improvement is made.

Each redundancy represents potential disaster for the family of the worker affected. Each redundancy has a very human cost in fear, stress and unhappiness, but it is the logic of money that the people making the redundancies are happy and that company is valued more highly every time this human tragedy is played out. In fact, each redundancy represents an opportunity for further profit or dividend for the business owners, and firms that can cut their payrolls in this way are often lauded in the business community.

Where it is not possible to make a position redundant many corporations choose to outsource work, in order to reduce their responsibilities to employees and reduce their committed cost base. This makes it easier to dump staff when they want and avoid the liabilities of employing people directly. The car manufacturing process has changed dramatically since the time of Henry Ford.[57] But employees continue to be hired, used and disposed of. They remain entirely helpless in managing or directing their own lives; our Egyptian scribe would be very pleased.

Technologies are not used to help people unless there is a profit to be made quickly, but used to replace people and fill us with fear for our livelihoods.

I remember watching television programmes in my youth which illustrated the lives we were expected to lead in the year 2001. I recall there were hover cars, every conceivable labour saving device, robot waiters and three hour working days predicted for us all.

Those Futurologists had made the mistake of thinking that mankind was free to make human decisions from an ethical perspective, where money was secondary to the needs of people.

In a monetary economy there is absolutely no incentive for a corporation or the social elite to make human and humane decisions; so we are offered distractions to stop us seeing our chains and feeling the whip. Whilst we live the way we do there is no hope that technology will serve us the way it should unless you are fortunate enough to be offered the chance to exchange your labour for tokens. People will always be subordinate to the drive for increased profit and will always need to be fearful that the next machine or device will rob them of their ability to feed themselves and their loved ones and keep a roof over their heads.

Our current economy is again facing yet another dead end with the way corporations handle technology. When a manufacturing innovation is made, it is not only the staff in the firm making the redundancies that is adversely affected; all the other manufacturers in that industry are adversely affected as well as their suppliers. If manufacturer A sheds 100 staff, their cost base goes down and the competition must respond in kind in order to remain competitive; their suppliers, service providers and outsourced workers find themselves with less business coming in. Soon you have a situation where thousands of people are losing their jobs with very little chance of finding a position that they are trained for and best able to maintain their standard of living with. The impact of this is of course homelessness for many and great distress for all. We are seeing this right now in the banking, motor vehicle, furnishing, property maintenance, retail, entertainment and house building sectors, each institution trying to dump as many employees as it can. With those redundancies it follows that the businesses that supplied these sectors are also forced to make redundancies of their own.

The impact on consumer choice is clear. The money society forces uniformity upon all but the most elite/bespoke of shoppers. Those firms that refuse to adopt the cheapest processes are often forced out of business or acquired by a larger competitor removing the choice to the community. We see this when we walk down the High Street or go to a shopping mall in any of our towns or cities. Towns are now virtually indistinguishable from each other, because before you get there you already know the choice of products that are available to you. This is even happening on an international stage. You can fly across the world and find the same fast food outlets, supermarkets and clothes shops waiting for you. Weren't we always told that capitalism encouraged choice?

There is further and perhaps more important damage caused by our current use of technology; with each innovation people lose their jobs and are forced to re-train and find employment in another field to have an opportunity of earning a living. As time passes the areas requiring human labour are reduced with each technical innovation. Therefore there are fewer jobs and huge numbers chasing them, each desperate to provide for themselves. There are machines now in development which will shortly replace the human surgeon; architects, train and taxi drivers, banking and retail administration and pilots are under threat and having seen the latest improvements in visual CGI technology even Actors have reason to be concerned.

It is inevitable that one day the system will implode because there will be so few in the position to earn and consume whilst paying taxes to support the huge numbers of people that are simply unable to find employment or need financial help in their old age. The exact point of economic collapse is virtually impossible to pin point and there are many factors that have great bearing, however a combination of unemployment, inflation, interest rates and national debt levels are considered among the key indicators of an economy in difficulties. Many industrialised nations are seeking to delay the inevitable by increasing the retirement from work ages, but we should be examining how we replace this system rather than prop it up.

If we do not change our relationship with technology it remains a matter of time before a money economy becomes entirely unsustainable.

8

Conclusion to Book One

Those who are too smart to engage in politics are punished by being governed by those that are dumber

— Plato

Our present method of self governance and group decision making is clearly not fit for current purpose. Our current methods are effectively unchanged from their pre-historic origins, sourced from uneducated, fearful, greedy, war-like and strictly hierarchical cultures, with methods appropriate to their technology levels and the low resources/technology available to them.

We have changed the titles of our leaders from Tribal Leaders to Pharoahs, to Monarchs to Presidents and Prime Ministers, Dictators and Politbureau's and more recently Director and CEO; yet the features and outcomes are effectively the same. The ruled have ineffective methods of influencing their leadership and resources are distributed as the leadership sees fit without regard for the needs of humans lower down the social ladder.

Our politics needs to adapt to the needs of a population and not just its elite.

Our present way of distributing resources is unfit for purpose. Where resources can be abundant it is obscene that a single child is hungry or a single adult sleeps rough through necessity.

This inevitable consequence of our current money economy requires us to plan a new way of distributing goods and services, so that we can have a planned and orderly transition to a new kind of economy.

Even without the Iceland scenario described in an earlier chapter our relationship and love affair with money must end. Capitalism and Socialism will eat itself; our system will one day collapse. We must change our dependence on money and give us and all our children a more stable, more equitable world, because there is no guarantee that our family will continue to be one of the few beneficiaries if we keep this failing system going into the future.

It is time we recognised that we have got the society we have complied with, looking away and keeping ourselves busy pleasing others for money that isn't even real; it's the thing we exchange for money that we want.

We can and must change this. We must stop supporting the institutions that have caused us so much misery and fear. It is time for us to take control and put a stop to the cruelties conducted in our name to people, animals and to the planet itself. Under a money system it will never stop, unless we stop it.

Together we can make change happen and make society reflect what we want. It need not be painful for us or too inconvenient, but if we all did a little it would soon change because we are many and they are so few. We have the power but the elite have control.

The world, the environment, animal life and people are ready for the first society driven by us; for the first time in human history – real change. No more pyramidal power structure – it's our turn. No more being victim to the failing logic of money.

Book 2. An alternative

9

A Different Way of Doing Things – Earth Economics The Earth's Ample Resources with Technology Humanely & Sustain-ably applied

As long as there is plenty, poverty is evil

– Robert F Kennedy

Earth economics is a modernised re-application of a very old way of living. It was practiced by indigenous Aboriginal, Native American and certain African societies before their technological and cultural progress was halted by interruption. These old societies had at their core, respect for nature, minimal waste-fulness, and the principal of freely sharing resources with humans in need. After all, it was the Native Americans that freely helped the early settlers survive their first harsh winters and accepted trinkets for land they thought they were being asked to share, rather than the land being fenced off and forbidden to them.

These old cultures were by no means perfect, were very tribal, with a strong hunting and ritual/stylised violent element that served to allow warriors to demonstrate their courage and physical prowess. There were inter-tribal conflicts; however, the purpose was usually around settling resource disputes such as the theft of food or around family/social issues such as the abduction of women. (There is evidence that some aboriginal groups settled inter-tribal conflict with singing and dancing contests in order to avoid actual violence).[58] However, within their own groups, they set aside differences and cared for each and every individual within the limits of the available resources, with no artificial constructs between what people needed and what they received.

The key point is that now our current level of technology allows us to bypass the bane of their society and ours – scarcity. Maybe we will be able to complete the cultural journey our more peaceful ancestors started out on, if we are mature enough?

The inadequacies of the current system are obvious. Criticism is easy and being constructive is much more difficult. But for the first time in human history we don't have the issue of how to allocate scarce resources; the resources are here and the technology exists to give every human an excellent standard of living.[59] Western and first world countries today have the capability of providing all of their homeless with a property, a personal vehicle and the means to obtain three well balanced meals each day, but for excellent economic reasons and because of potential resistance from people that enjoy witnessing human misery, they choose not to.

The wealthy countries could halt all property repossessions, but they choose not to for excellent economic reasons and because it would also upset those that pay their mortgages, regardless of how they obtain that money. The first world countries could make meaningful and permanent change in the most poverty stricken countries but choose not to for excellent economic reasons.

The profit motive and money system is no longer appropriate because it addresses issues of scarcity that no longer exist and is now responsible for the terrible inequalities of this world, propping up the people that make the awful decisions under which we suffer.

The current economy does not encourage intelligent use of the Earth's resources to meet the needs of the environment, people and animals. We are all too often victim to the drive for immediate profit and short term thinking. Always someone, somewhere is paying in unrewarded labour or human misery while another reaps the profit.

The obsolete resource distribution method of money can now be replaced with something that treats all humans with dignity. The neo feudal system we live under must end.

Earth Economics is a system where resources are intelligently managed for the good of all. There is no profit driven corporations or individuals capable of holding back the interests of the community at large and no vested interests to protect. There is no one making short term, profit driven decisions that others have to pay for; no intrigue to maintain privileged business or political positions and no instigating wars in order to benefit share or stock holders. Decisions are jointly made purely based upon what is best for people and the planet – absolutely nothing else. The reason for this is there is no money acting as a motivator for action and as a method of rationing resources among those that have the right tokens, leaving those without cash outside of the bounty available and unable to have their equally important human needs met.

The principal of Earth Economics is briefly as follows:

Resources are collected in an environmentally sustainable manner. Manufacturing processes are designed to require minimal human labour with environmental sustainability being the highest concern. All available technical innovations/inventions/ideas are reviewed for benefit to humankind and environmental concerns. These ideas are then implemented after being checked for resource requirement versus benefit to all people, not one person left out. It is not forgotten that the planet provides the resources for every human endeavour and that each human has the same physical needs. This is achieved by conducting a worldwide inventory of resources; natural, technological and intellectual.[60] These audits are conducted against a background of understanding the environmental impact of obtaining and working with these materials and offsetting the impact when it is appropriate to do so. Native American cultures are understood to access the impact of any action to the seventh generation and have often said that if they had stewardship of our planet that it would still be possible to safely drink water from our streams and rivers.[61]

Preproduction, manufacturing, goods and service distribution processes are designed to require the minimum of human labour. When human labour is required, work does not devolve onto the shoulders of a few overworked and stressed individuals that have had to complete for the opportunity to provide for their families. Work schedules are distributed among those that are capable, competent and who wish to contribute in that area. Goods are distributed not through a money rationing process, but as a result of an assessment and agreement on the standard of living that each citizen should have. This agreement being arrived at by democratic consensus processes. The expected standard of living need be the only political decision that needs to be made by society.

The intension is for poorer regions of the earth to catch up with the richer areas, but for practical reasons that may not happen overnight, although providing food and basic amenities would be virtually instantaneous.

We would work towards providing every human with the following, freely, without obligation to another person:

A comfortable, environmentally powered home.
Respectfully reared or healthily grown foods.
A choice of clothing manufactured without cruelty.
Education and healthcare.
Various entertainments, including recreation and leisure.
Personal and public transport.
A humane society will work to ensure that every human benefits from the resources available and lives with the dignity that being human deserves.

Basically, I am proposing updating the key principals of a truly ancient and humane way of managing human affairs. It is only now that the technology exists to make it work in a global manner, without reducing anyone's standard of living and improving the lifestyle of the majority of the world. Instead of nations in competition with each other, seeking advantages; are we not now mature enough to have nations work together to address the issue of resource scarcity and improve life for all whilst addressing environmental issues or do our leaders have different agendas?

With people focussed politics, humanity can step up to the next developmental stage in civilisation and set aside its childish cruelties.

As we have seen a method of resource distribution based on rationing by money, rather than rationing based on resource availability is clearly failing to achieve the clear objective of satisfying universal human need.

10

What Would Earth Economics Mean to People?

To be free is not merely to cast off one's chains, but to live in a way that respects and enhances the freedom of others.

Nelson Mandela

If nations worked together with a mature respect for human dignity, the world would be transformed and become a place fit for our children and grandchildren to inherit.

We only need the emotional maturity to let our current system go, where it will be viewed with the same distain as we view witch burnings, human sacrifice and feudal servitude. How we live now is primitive, inhumane, unsustainable, short sighted and quite foolish.

The best way to illustrate the effect of change is to examine the key areas of life as it affects people and discuss them point by point.

Personal Life:
Every human would be provided with the requisites of life without charge, obligation or having to exchange labour or possessions for them. Goods and services can be ordered online and through distribution centres similar to our existing shops and malls, whilst automated processes and volunteers provide the labour. This would free people to pursue the tasks, activities and education they love, the results of these activities being freely available to the community, just as the voluntary activities of others are freely available to us. People will be freed from the burden of worrying about money and will have more personal

time to build better and stronger relationships. Under this system we are freed from many of the stresses we currently take for granted, able to make decisions about our relationships without the influence that money often has over us. We would have the time to be more thoughtful, considerate, mature and relaxed in our dealings. It would foster a true honesty in all our contacts because we would have nothing to gain by behaviours rooted in the logic of money.

Removing money would allow people to achieve status and respect "through the content of their character" and their positive achievements rather than the false cache given by cash in the bank or the car they drive. The status conferred by money can be achieved by corrupt and inhuman means, by trading narcotics, weapons and other means of killing people, by choosing the right lottery numbers or by being born into a wealthy family.

Friendships and dealings would be truly genuine; human interactions would have no element of seeking advantage over another, or concern that someone is seeking advantage. There would be no forced dominance or control over another person and the financial inequalities in relationships so often seen would disappear. People would be free to pursue their lives truly in accordance with their conscience and convictions – for the first time able to respect another person totally without fear or favour and receive the same.

Personal Behaviours

A criticism put to me about Earth Economics is current human behaviours. We see people trampling each other to secure a bargain in a sale. If a commodity is rumoured to be in short supply (like vehicle fuel) immediately we see queues of people panic buying. We hear stories of people panic buying and either profiteering or hoarding their surplus.[62]

The root cause of these behaviours is fear of scarcity and the idea that we are in competition with our neighbours and must therefore seek advantage. In a money economy these unproductive behaviours are actually logical, although they often cause the feared shortages and result in unhappiness, resentments and stress.

These activities are currently logical because we must ensure our limited purchasing power is used in the most effective way possible. If extending our personal purchasing power means barging someone frailer out of the way (for example, when a shop discounts its prices) then that is the natural consequence of an economy predicated upon an assumption of scarcity. That minor scuffle is actually good business for both the victor and the vendor.

If we can offer a product or service to society, a money economy obliges us to squeeze every last possible penny from the individual that needs it, regardless of the hardship caused and the circumstances of the buyer.

An Earth based economy directly addresses these undesirable behaviours that are currently logical, understandable, encouraged and indeed necessary for personal survival. Removing the imperative to maximise limited purchasing power and the opposing incompatible drive to maximise profit removes the need for people to compete with their neighbour.

Ensuring the requisites of life are freely available without obligation will create a sense of abundance from which a true spirit of community and sharing would grow.[62] There would be no need to hoard or practice any other anti-social behaviours rooted in the failing logic of money.

The sense of scarcity that we live with is now false. It is a construct to maintain a failing order, benefit those that lead it and enforce our obedience. The concept of scarcity is now outdated, we just have to recognise it. If you need evidence, look at the millions of empty houses, the acres of unsold new vehicles being stored at dockyards,[63] the food and clothes we discard or see warehoused.

Work and Career

The face of work would be transformed.

Working for the benefit of those at the top of the corporation pyramid, for minimal compensation, living in fear of being discarded for another person or a machine would be a thing of the past. There would be no need to accept a job that depresses or is hated in order to have food to eat and somewhere to live.

Young people would not have to give their most vigorous years completing mindless tasks for minimal pay because they need the money, and mature people wouldn't need to sell their precious and limited time in order to support their human needs.

People would be free to choose the area of work they wish to be involved with, contributing to society within their capabilities and commitments and making the results freely available to others. Automation would be used to benefit all peoples, so instead of the earlier mentioned car factory making cars only for those that can pay; it would produce cars for those that want one.

Tasks would be completed in the spirit of cooperation among colleagues, with work loads spread among more people who genuinely want to be there. Automatically there would be a better, more productive working environment because we would no longer be afraid of our bosses; the work routine would better reflect our outside needs and gentle working hours, etc, would allow for more vigorous engagement with work.

This way of working immediately destroys the subservience of hierarchy; it frees people to speak when things are going wrong and allows management to react to problems without fear for their livelihoods.[64] This would remove so many of the wasteful practices and occurrences that happen today, that management isn't necessarily aware of. A good example comes from my personal experience: My first full-time job was for a major employer. After a week or so, another employee took me aside to tell me I was working too hard and too quickly, making him and the rest look bad. He told me that they were not paid enough to consistently put that kind of effort in and that I would cause problems for everyone else if I continued. He was very friendly, but the message was clear. He also showed me how to appear busy and how to use the system to my advantage. Of course, I took his advice. I stayed there several years (because I needed the money) until boredom and unhappiness drove me away.

This scenario is being played out all over the planet, with employers designing work environments that become more oppressive or pressuring staff to work longer hours than is ideal[65] (ensuring maximum work for the wages paid) and employees respond by seeking ways of coping with their unhappy work-life. Employees often express their frustration by giving resentful service to their employers and clients, whilst others develop emotional issues such as depression or stress related illness. Professor Cary Cooper, Lancaster University Management School, said: 'Employers should seriously look at tackling the consequences of job dissatisfaction and related health problems with innovative policies'.

All these issues further serve to highlight the minor differences that we have, guaranteeing 'them and us' situations, even when we are trying to achieve the same goals.

Another example of waste is the individual offered a promotion away from a job he enjoyed doing and in which he was very effective. He accepts promotion because he needs the extra money, but finds himself to be less happy and the corporation loses an effective employee to a position where he could be less effective.

There is the question of whether anything would be achieved without money as an incentive. Research conducted by human resource professionals[66] shows that compensation is not necessarily the best way of retaining happy staff.

We can all think of individuals who have achieved monetary success and who continue to work. Many of these people are no longer motivated by money but by the drive to be creative, have their talent recognised, be respected, be challenged, for authority or simply to prevent boredom. In business there are a number of financially independent people called 'business angels' who work on projects that interest them for no guaranteed financial return. All people should be able to work this way, not just the wealthy.

There are people who continue to work because they have pride in the quality of their work; they are craftsmen, love what they do and love to teach others. Earth Economics will allow everybody the pleasure of doing only what they wish without pressure. Naturally, people would be happier, more productive and much better placed to release their natural human potential and help drive innovation and improvement of life for us all.

11

What Would Earth Economics Mean to Society?

Almost always the creative dedicated minority has made the world better

Dr Martin Luther King Jr

Wider society will be transformed and better able to address human needs. There are many institutions we are familiar with today that will simply disappear, and others that can for the first time operate without concern for financial budgets.

Our current pyramidal social structure will be transformed into a flat configuration with no tiny elite owning the resources needed by all people. This would mean that decisions are taken without regard to the interests of a powerful few, without possibility of corruption and not subject to short term thinking.

Again, we'll look at each area of public life and discuss them point by point:

Politics

The impact on politics would be dramatic. The present distinctions of left and right would become obsolete because there's only one decision for people to democratically make; what should the standard of living be for every human and how quickly can the agreed quality of life be achieved?

Once the universal standard of living has been democratically decided by the people, there is no need for further political debate and logically, no need for politicians, only able administrators and organisers. The result of that single debate in which we set our priorities and expectations serves as an instruction to government. We would have bottom-up leadership (rather than top-down), where people decide how the Earths resources are to be used to our benefit.

Politics would lose its power of patronage, influence and control and would, therefore, stop attracting personalities interested only in personal power. It would lose its potential for intrigue, hypocrisy, childish point scoring and its mysterious lack of transparency, because there is literally only one objective, which is set by the people.

This future society will reach its decisions bearing in mind that we should never accept something for someone else that we wouldn't accept for ourselves. Government would purely serve society and the people would see clearly whether the objectives set are being delivered in a sustainable way.

This change in direction for politics is likely to revive people's interest in the political process.[67]

We would no longer elect people to have power over us that we cannot control or oppose once in office. We would end the tyranny of the ballot box.

Abraham Lincoln once said 'no man is good enough to govern another man without the others consent'. Under our money-based economy we are clearly not being governed to our benefit, the wars and the suffering is not something we consented to. Even George W Bush agrees with me when he said 'free nations don't develop weapons of mass destruction'; he goes even further: 'The constitution is just a god-damn piece of paper'. This further indicates the esteem in which our leaders hold us.

Government

The face and goals of government change beyond recognition. Government becomes a coordinating body ensuring that human needs are met to the standard agreed on a political level. The principal responsibilities would be providing self-directed educational opportunities, natural resource management, commissioning of essential production, distribution and delivery of other essential services, law enforcement and the sustainable and respectful management of fish, crops, environment and animal stock.

The process of government would be comparable to the civil service; an administrations function without policy decisions to make, but clear targets to achieve. Obviously, there is no concern for money budgets or restrictive vested interests, just ensuring the goods and services we demand are delivered, without harm to people or environment.

The task of government devolves to true public servants who have no authority to instigate wars, spy on our activities or order any activity that was not expressly decided by people at the political level. This would mean that government could not make any changes in our rights and obligations without our express direction.

Competent administrators would be democratically selected, after examination of their achievements (no campaigning rallies and cults of personality) to serve a pre-determined term of service. The Administration team would be prohibited from any involvement in the political decision making process (being there only to serve and deliver our instructions). The administration team should also be excluded from any relationship with media, law enforcement or any other civic service that society needs; thus restricting government influence and ensuring absolute independence of all the key institutions.

Government would no longer be about leadership; it is about satisfying a directive from the populace. The purpose of government becomes clear and transparent. It also becomes very simple for the community to identify who are poor or able administrators and dismiss them if they are not delivering the group instructions given by us.

War

Because resources are freely exchanged and the use of renewable energy technologies is maximised, there is no inclination to acquire the territory of another by force. Additionally, government would have the authority to instigate and conduct war removed, only doing what government should do in a civilised society – represent its people's wishes.

Furthermore, without the whip of money there would be virtually no one prepared to kill and be killed. With the needs of people freely met it is unlikely that war could physically happen because people wouldn't have to join the armed services to support themselves and their families, and professional killing would no longer be acceptable in the new civilisation.

Divisions between people would fade because we would all be co-dependent. We already are, but the current financial system masks this with its adversarial progresses that force people to fear, compete and join up with opposing groups and views. People would also have the time to truly consider the issues before committing to any aggressive actions.

Arms manufacturers would find themselves without labour and anyone who tried to use the Earth's resources in such a destructive manner would find themselves ostracised, isolated and unable to ferment the troubles that provide them with profit, power and prestige today.

There would be no need for state sponsored violence and killing to further 'old world' political aims; and there would be no way of fermenting it. There would also not be any incentive towards terrorist action since the perceived injustices that motivate these acts would stop.

Education and its Application

The governments of all first world countries now devote a lot of time and resources to educating their citizens; government sets standardised learning expectations then put our children through a battery of tests to assess how much that child can recall. Original thinking or unconventional approaches to learning and problem solving are gently, but consistently discouraged.

Currently we have our education driven by the needs of employers (who regularly influence the syllabus we follow). We surrender our true interests for educational programmes focused around what makes us attractive to corporations who can later discard us if/when we are no longer useful or our experience no longer needed.

At Christmas, during the school play season, our young children are encouraged to sing about shopping and consuming along with carols, whilst wearing clothes sponsored by big business. Our children and we are systematically conditioned to become good consumers, judging each other by how much and how conspicuously we spend, whilst so many people in other countries literally eat cow dung to stay alive.

Education would be focused around teaching to the interests of the pupil, rather than teaching to a career choice that may no longer be relevant when it is time to start a career; talk to glass blowers, telex operators, bus conductors, type/print setters and other near-obsolete professions.[68] Removing the need to earn money would free people to follow their interests and where they have the talent, increase the pool of human knowledge.

Technological innovation, scientific and philosophical thinking would no longer be limited to a tiny group of privately financed individuals who have passed the filtering process. Now all talented people would have equal opportunity under this system to contribute. It is likely that humankind would experience a 'golden age' of development and improvement.

A study by Bowles, Samuel, Gintis and Herbert (The Inheritance of Inequality) found that the financial status of an individual's parents is a better indicator of eventual success than innate intelligence of the child (George W. Bush is an ideal example of this).[69] That finding has an untold impact on the whole of humankind.

A genius born in the wrong country, into the wrong family, has little chance of making the impact that his talent deserves. It is for this reason that less than 4 per cent of people are responsible for all the changes that people have seen over the centuries.

Many of the world's most intelligent and talented people have had to subordinate their creative talent to the need to earn enough money to keep body and soul together or please a wealthy patron (Michelangelo, Tesla and many more). And the poorer the community they are born into, the less time and opportunity they have to express their creativity or find a patron.

Look at Thomas Edison: He is recognised as inventing the first electric light bulb; it is little known that he made 10,000 mistakes before making one that worked reliably. Not many people would have been able to pursue such a worthy project through failure after failure. Edison's obsession and drive to achieve had to be matched by his financial capability; without this he could not have accomplished this important innovation.

How many of us could afford to follow our obsession in this way? How much human potential has been lost to us all?

Some people currently aspire to well-rewarded positions, such as doctors, etc, because they wish to help people and give themselves priority access to available resources. They are in-affect competing for what they perceive to be scarce resources, with society benefiting from the by-product of their efforts. Our current system restricts the number of doctors or other high achievers to those that pass the following four stage filtering process:

1. Desire
2. Aptitude
3. Effort and concentration
4. The ability to support oneself financially through nearly

ten years of study and internship.

This last represents an insuperable obstacle to many in achieving this goal, even if they possess all the other attributes. In fact, the other qualities count for nothing unless there is money to back them up. Yet a poor but financially independent student can achieve this goal or any other.

Changing the economy frees people from the concerns of personally scarce resources. An aspiring doctor no longer has to experience hardships during training, then demand huge financial compensation for the sacrifices they were obliged to make. There will not be an excessive workload or burdensome responsibilities waiting for them, neither is there any shortage of goods and services during or when their training is over. This would mean that the new society would benefit from the contributions of any/all high achievers. There is nothing that would obstruct their ability to improve the standard of living of the entire community.

Earth economics would unleash the untapped potential in every human and free each person to pursue their obsession, their bliss, and realise their creative dream without restraint, concern for or approval of the vested interests of a tiny social elite.

Imagine human potential without any shackles.

Crime

Crime within society is a source of so much pain and anxiety but under the economy proposed, the motivation for most crime would disappear immediately. Dr Chandre Gould of The Crime, Justice and Politics Programme (Pretoria) found that 68 per cent of adults in crime-ridden South Africa thought greed and genuine need was the motivating factor for crime.

The immediate elimination of crimes such as robbery and mugging is obvious, because there is literally nothing to gain from that behaviour. The impact is profound. People would be able to walk through any neighbourhood without fear of attack for their personal possessions. The elderly in particular would have no reason to feel fear and there is no reason to regard another group of people with suspicion. We are currently living in fear of youths in face concealing headwear called 'hoodies'. The clothing is merely a fashion which will pass like all others, but in a money economy, there is criminal advantage in it which some abuse. So, we walk in fear of all youth so attired, spreading division and dehumanising them, devoting newspaper space and television time to 'the problem with our youth',[70] when it is our society that has the problem.

But there is a deeper more cleansing effect of changing the structure of our economy.

A street drug dealer that spreads unhappiness destroys families, drives crime and degradation as his customers struggle to pay for his services; approximately 75 per cent of users commit crimes to feed their habit.[71] His wares cause women and boys to prostitute and arm themselves to deal with the dangerous situations they put themselves in. Further to that, the dealer needs to resolve turf disputes with other dealers often with fatal force, which increasingly innocent bystanders are harmed by. It is a terrible, fear-filled, violent and increasingly short life. Why does the dealer do it? As a child, was that really the life he wanted for himself?

Unfortunately, in a financial economy there will always be that loathsome dealer, because there will always be someone desperate enough to risk his life, sell out his personal dreams, risk the shame of his parents and sell out his human integrity for the need to get money, by fair means or foul. The dealer will always be there to supply a demand and bring harm to the wider community.

Think about this: Under our current system there will always be people desperate enough to pimp, prostitute, push drugs on our children, rob us with violence, steal from our homes, defraud us, con and deceive us, intimidate our elderly for the resources they need to sustain themselves and their families. It will never ever stop because they must satisfy their own human needs even at cost to others; we can't expect these people to simply lie down and die.

But that street dealer is the last link in a chain of pain and cruelty. The narcotics he deals have passed through so many hands on their journey to our streets from such places as Afghanistan or Columbia. The government spends money locking up the small dealer but the real kingpins making the big profits are left alone to enjoy their fabulous lifestyles. Is this because the key figures are rich enough to buy protection from the law?

This idea is not as absurd as it initially sounds. There are historical models that fit and still apply because our societies are fundamentally the same despite the passage of time.

The British East India Company was granted a Royal Charter and monopoly privileges and it traded in various forms until January 1874.[72] The company was licensed to rule a large proportion of India. Among the many respectable products it was involved with, it traded opium. The East India Company gave large quantities of opium free to China's people in a 'try before you buy' promotional marketing campaign. The addictive and de-habilitating effects soon became obvious and the Chinese government moved to make the drug illegal in 1729. Despite China's attempts to protect its people, the corporation continued to push opium. In 1840 and 1858 the British government waged war, defeating the Chinese military twice to protect its drug dealer, its turf and tax revenues.

More recently, Professor Alfred McCoy[73] provided evidence that an American Government Agency (the CIA) traded Opium during the Vietnam War years.

In November 1993, Judge Robert Bonner appeared on

American television[74] and alleged that the CIA had permitted literally a ton of cocaine to enter the United States. He alleged it may not be an isolated incident.

There are a number of writers on this subject making some devastating observations. This is all inevitable in a money-based economy; it is the logic of money. It is with wry amusement that I note governments in Britain and America talking about being 'tough on crime and tough on the causes of crime'. While there is money to be made it will never be wiped out, whether our governments are behind it (as is alleged by many) or if individuals in key positions have been corrupted. Our question now becomes: Is there a place for narcotics in Earth Economics?

The factors that motivate an individual to experiment with drugs and develop an addiction are not fully understood. There are questions around environment, rebellion, thrill-seekers and risk-takers and those that retreat to drug use in order to escape their problems, which often results in a vicious circle.

Therefore, under the new system, the motivation for an unknown proportion of people to use drugs will disappear, because we will not be subject to many of the stresses that we live with today. Although there may still be a demand for narcotics, the real question is what is the impact of these users in this new economy?

If individuals within society choose to make narcotics available, the user is no longer driven to crime to maintain their habit. There is no advantage in crime for money and the addict is now unable to reduce his dependents to poverty. The destructive impact is massively reduced to antisocial behaviours, which society will be much better placed to deal with. Removing the profit removes the urge of otherwise good people to supply these harmful substances, there is simply no profit, no point.

Under the new economy, the only crimes that may continue would be those of a personal or relationship nature.

However, even these are likely to diminish because people

will have more time to mature and think about the issues in their lives. They will no longer be financially tied to another person and are better placed to manage their relationships. We now see murders for inheritances, for insurance, for business advantage, among couples that wish to keep the relationship's financial assets – all these problems disappear.

We currently see so many examples of greedy selfishness and other fear based behaviours that many wonder if these human weaknesses will make this proposal unworkable.

The real issue is whether human behaviour is programmed and pre-determined, rendering the will of the individual irrelevant or whether people are responsible for their own actions and able to address issues in their character that may be undesirable.

Studies are showing that behaviour is an expression of the following combination of factors: the customs of the society we are born into, personality, conditioning, peer groups and social control factors.[75] This implies human behaviour is malleable and adjusts with circumstances, social expectation, environment, etc. This is clearly the case. Only a few hundred years ago public executions were considered as good wholesome family entertainment in Britain and other countries with current social care pretensions. Children were employed at dangerous and often fatal tasks and personal hygiene was considered unnecessary.

More recently, it is no longer possible to find racist mainstream television programming such as *The Black & White Minstrel Show*, neither is it acceptable to openly express similar attitudes. If people were not capable of change we would execute people for stealing food, sacrifice virgins and rush to amphitheatres to watch lions eating Christians, indeed we would not have left our caves.

Human behaviours change as the social environment change; therefore, society can change and often has. If we provide people with an environment where there is no fear of having needs met, then fear-based behaviours will quickly recede.

Law & Law Enforcement

The legal system and law enforcement would also change irrevocably.

These agencies will be independent of government and tasked with implementing the expectations of society only. It is likely there will be less need for a full code of law, which currently seeks to control most aspects of people's behaviour through a framework of structured punishments.

Making full use of implemented technologies would take care of most misdemeanours.

For example, it is against the law to operate a vehicle under the influence of alcohol and now much resource is spent educating people against it, educating law enforcement to recognise it and arrest the suspected individuals. That individual may cause loss of life or property bringing distress to many and then further resources are expended taking that offender to trial where he may be subject to incarceration or be obliged to accept a driving education programme; this is all very wasteful and unnecessary.

The technology exists to have the vehicle simply not work if the driver has alcohol in their breath (and shortly cars will auto pilot making driver competence irrelevant and taxi drivers redundant), saving so much time, distress to society and unnecessary work'.[76] When technology is used in this way so many human misdemeanours become simply impossible, freeing resources for more important priorities.

Another example is graffiti; this can be completely eradicated by simply using a coating that cannot be marked. Technology can be used in a way to simply eliminate many issues currently dealt with by law and statutes, law enforcement and court.

Naturally, these simple solutions are impossible to implement in a money system because there is always the question of who will pay rather than if it can be done. In the meantime, people are suffering and more resources are expended in the end, punishing and criminalising people that act in these preventable manners and rectifying unnecessary damage to property.

Religion

The focus of religion will change from helping people make sense of the pressures of everyday life to helping people develop their spirituality.

Removing profit and money would remove the incentive for religious institutions to cheerlead for political decisions and secular organisations. The ridiculous situation of religious leaders on both side of a war, calling on God's blessing and support for killing the other, would be over.

The religions would adapt to deal purely with the spirituality of their own members, helping their followers recognise the humanity and worthiness of each individual human, using their influence to support peace and love; the genuinely civilised qualities.[77]

People would be freed to think about the nature of their faith and we would hope that the new mantra of 'only accept for others what you would accept for yourself' is adopted in the religions of the coming world order.

People would be freed from the prejudices of others to follow their religious convictions, because it is what we would want for ourselves. Religion would adapt to respect the humanity of those practicing other faiths and not involve itself in destructive competition with other cultures. It should be noted that an individual's religion is most often a result of the family and culture into which they have been born. It is their family tradition, if you will. It is not a reason for war and conflict.

The Media

Journalism and the media would continue to be an essential

component of ensuring society knows that the administrators/ government are doing their job correctly and that they are held to account in the event of failures to achieve the tasks we set for them. It is therefore important that the 'forth estate' (media) is independent and structured in such a way that it avoids any influence from government, individuals, corporations, lobbyists or special interest groups or for its leaders to become entrenched.

Making the media into something that cannot be owned or controlled protects the integrity of this institution and would ensure that people receive truly impartial information from journalists that cannot benefit from representing a biased view.

Technology assists in this function because vigilant people are able to inform the public independently of any failures that may otherwise by covered up. This structure would allow society to ensure that each human is treated in a manner that we would accept for ourselves, protecting the rights of each individual.

Earth Economics & Food:

Removing the pressure for profit will remove the pressure for intense/cruel or unkind animal rearing. It will eliminate the desirability of genetically modified foods (the health conse- quences of which are entirely unknown) and the need for the more harmful pesticides. There would be no benefit to anyone in providing sub-standard and dangerous foods, and technology can be applied to ensure we get the best possible sustenance.

For example, soil quality in terms of nutrient levels, etc, can now be monitored by sensors, so computers can calculate what needs to be added to the soil to ensure that people receive the best possible nutrients and automation supplies the labour where possible.[78]

The same environmental priorities will also be applied to our husbandry of the sea, its food and its other resources.

The current system often penalises countries for growing the crops they are best suited for and most efficient at. A good example of this is the tea growing regions of Sri Lanka. Tea is used virtually worldwide giving much pleasure to many people. However, whilst Sri Lanka has an 'absolute advantage[79] in producing this crop and is more effective at growing it over, say, France, this commodity is not particularly highly valued in money terms. Therefore, the farmers working with this crop will always struggle financially because the terms of trade are against them.[80] This means that a tea grower must sell major quantities of his product to earn enough to buy a car, (even though cars are plentiful) meaning that a car is hugely expensive for them even though they provide a product that so many people enjoy. This tea grower will always remain impoverished.

Under a money system we are actually in danger of losing this product. Let us imagine that the soil and climate there is discovered as highly advantageous for a petroleum replacement product, the price of which is ten times the amount paid for tea. How long would it be before tea either disappeared or became an expensive luxury?

This very scenario is actually happening now. Because of the collapse in coffee prices, Ethiopian growers are replacing their socially responsible product with an illegal narcotic called chat or khat (which is an amphetamine and highly additive).[81] Ethiopia has been connected with coffee growing for 3,000 years but because its growers can no longer make a living from growing it, OXFAM (a British based international charity) estimates that khat will become Ethiopia's largest export within ten years.[82]

Again, Peruvian coffee growers are increasingly turning to cultivating the precursor for cocaine because they do not have a means of supporting themselves; because they need the money.

You will not be surprised to find that there are four major western based coffee buying corporations who between them set the purchasing price.[83] These corporations have done nothing but acquire this crop at the best possible price, which makes good business sense. However, someone must always pay for a cheaply acquired item and it is the often third world growers that are paying with their under-rewarded labour.

Whilst the farmers change their production from the crops that decent society wants, to illegal and harmful goods, the farmers are inadvertently harming the environment and consuming their new produce to have the physical strength to 'slave' inhuman hours and quell their hunger pangs.

My point is that money is a poor way of deciding and distributing the needs of people and even worst at ensuring that we get it.

Commodity growers of products similar to tea, coffee, etc, also deserve a human standard of living and should not suffer for providing us with their socially responsible produce.

Earth Economics will ensure more variety and more security of choice for us, because no one is penalised for creating a desired and desirable product with poor terms of trade.

We would see land used in the most effective and naturally sympathetic method possible, in the appropriate regions (measured by comparative or absolute advantage analysis) to maximise food and other production. We would find that the world would become significantly more efficient at sustaining all human life if nations cooperated with each other rather than competed.

Medicine

Our medical institutions would be revitalised by removing the need to make profit. In the UK we have sick patients given non optimal treatments because of the cost of medicine rather than the ability to heal. Those with the ability to pay receive the best possible attention, despite our National Health system claiming that good health care is a right for all our citizens, whilst in America the problem is hugely worse.

Instead of the bulk of research going into profitable on-going treatments, our medical industry will be motivated to cure human health problems and not just the high profile and profitable ones. In the New World Order, this industry will only ever implement the best options available.

People would be freed to contribute to the sum of human knowledge. More people with more time, with a protected environment, sympathetically studied, are highly likely to generate many solutions to human problems. It should also be remembered that the new economy will improve base levels of health. Our governments already acknowledge that the vegetables that we currently buy are no longer capable of sustaining optimal health.

Pregnant women are now advised to take folic acid daily supplements to avoid birth defects. Folic acid used to be plentiful in green vegetables with the essential trace mineral selenium, without which our bodies struggle to preserve natural good health.[84] These virtually disappeared from our soil and crops approximately 50 years ago.[85]

Cancer Research UK said in December 2004, that childhood cancers have increased to 0.8 per cent year on year since 1962 and are implying that food quality is a significant contributor to this trend. We have seen burgeoning rates of autism and the emergence of new illnesses like M.E, and heart disease which were unheard of 110 years ago.[85] We now have reason to believe that our deteriorating water quality is changing the sex of certain fish and reducing male fertility.

A profitless society would make a huge step to improving human health, purely by ensuring the quality of the food we consume. In combination with a genuine effort to cure health issues we would see the quality of life improve immeasurably for humankind.

How Technology Will be Used:

Currently technology is a source of fear to many people trying to earn a living and a great advantage to business owners who seek to reduce their labour costs. This situation is entirely counterproductive and foolish. Technology is filtered through the interests of corporations before it has an opportunity to serve humankind.

The only filters for technology will be environmental impact, whether it contributes to the quality of people's live and if manufacture can be achieved by robot. It will be important that it reduces the need for human labour in its application and assumes tasks essential for sustaining a quality lifestyle.

The drive of technology will be to automate as many tasks as possible, removing the need for humans to labour, freeing people to realise their true potentials rather than working for the benefit of a corporation.

This approach will be used to address the issues important to humankind. In the future, machines will create homes, from materials better able to deal with the issues of weather, etc, which we face.

Imagine unleashed imagination and wonderful solutions to problems that are just impossible in a money-based society. Our current money society must always look backward for the financially prudent and proven way before being able to act to change anything, often bypassing the inspired solution.

Transport

This area of life is responsible for so much environmental damage and will be radically different under Earth Economics.

The first change is that the 'rush hour' will disappear. There will be no need to transport millions of people into and out of commercial centres at the same time, causing gridlock and misery for the commuters. This gridlock is highly wasteful of resources and totally unnecessary.

Without profit-driven corporations to obstruct effective but unprofitable technology, methods of transport will be changed for more environmentally sustainable methods virtually overnight. For example, the technology exists today to provide us with vehicles that travel 220 miles on a single electrical charge and provide virtually super car performance in silence.[86]

For longer journeys we have Maglev train technology which is capable of extreme high speed whilst consuming a fraction of the energy of a conventional train.[87] With further development, Maglev technology will be capable of replacing commercial air travel once environmentally acceptable tunnels similar to the English Tunnel are dug. This technology is highly efficient, very environmentally desirable and ready for us to use now. It has not been done, not because it is impossible but, because the costs outweigh the projected profits; the fact that the earth dies without it does not enter the equation. Those that can pay for improving the world in this and other ways simply chose not to – they choose to fight wars instead.

Energy Needs

We are currently burning gas, oil and coal, which release CO_2 gases into the atmosphere; we risk nuclear meltdown, use incinerators and other dirty methods to power our lives.

We live in a bountiful world but the logic is such that even in prosperous countries people suffer or die for lack of money, when what they need is literally there to be used.

In the UK every winter a terrible tragedy plays out year after year. The elderly often living on a fixed income (eroded by inflation), find they do not have sufficient cash to pay their winter heating bills, eat and clothe themselves. Because they have to manage their limited cash, too many of our grandparents and senior citizens die each year through fear of the utility bill. And for every death caused by fear of a utility bill, there are several cases where people avoid heating their home by riding public transport or visiting public buildings all day in order to stay warm.

Think about this:

This individual dies slowly of hypothermia whilst there is a perfectly operational gas and electricity supply to their home, but their fear of not being able to pay overrides their fear of discomfort; this means that the individual feels unable to turn the heating on and many don't.[88]

Meanwhile, the energy corporations make huge profit for their warm owners and issue statements to the media stating that payment plans were available to the elderly if the person concerned had taken the trouble to telephone them, navigate their complicated telephone systems and explain their circumstances, which would then be subject to assessment by an employee who is required to apply a rigid process to the caller.

And we call ourselves civilised.

The British government has fairly recently started paying a modest winter fuel bonus to the elderly, but this does very little to address the issue our seniors face, because the bonus payment just disappears into all the other costs and taxes of life.

Again, this is no longer necessary.

Efficient and low consumption machinery could be used to compliment the bountiful, clean and freely available wind, wave and solar energy. We also currently have geothermic energy available and the future promises zero point and piezoelectric energy and other technologies, which would provide people with all the energy they could possibly need – all freely available. All of this is currently held back (by way of under investment) whilst the corporations frantically work out ways to charge us for using them.

Today we could design homes that provide free energy to the occupants that need it, all without charge, merely for being a human being. Our vehicles could be free to run and much more efficient than we experience now, but they are not because there is profit to be made from selling, servicing, fuelling and maintaining our old polluting vehicles.

12

Conclusion to Book 2

New ideas pass through three periods: 1) It can't be done. 2) It probably can be done, but it's not worth doing. 3) I knew it was a good idea all along.

Arthur C Clark

Earth economics combined with a new politics, would clearly address the issues of being human in a holistic, sustainable and intelligent manner.

It would end the cruelties and divisions that we currently fabricate and usher in a genuine and sustainable golden age.

But there is yet an essential question.

Can society change and how do we bring change about?

Book Three: How to get there

13

Can Society Change?

Every civilization that has ever existed has ultimately collapsed.

Henry Kissenger

It is all well and good talking about earth economics but as I write each of us has to deal with the daily difficulties of life in a money system. As we look at our bills and worry about how to pay them, it all seems so far away and our problems so deeply entrenched that there can be no hope of achieving such a wonderful new life, sparing our children and grandchildren the problems we face today.

Well, society has changed over time and this change is possible.

Historically, there have been several huge upheavals in society over the years. a few being (in no particular order):

1. Magna Carta
2. Women's Suffrage
3. Emancipation of the black African slave
4. The American Civil Rights Movement
5. The French Revolution
6. The Russian Revolution
7. The provision of pension and health care rights for workers.

All of these events have represented important changes in the social evolution of the human world and helped influence the lives we lead today in the West.

As important as these changes have been, there remains

something untouched that must be addressed before a genuine new world can be born.

Those changes have tinkered around the edges of the true problem and not dealt with the heart of the matter. A good example of this is Germany under the stanch Royalist Chancellor Otto von Bismarck in the 1870's. His party was losing ground to the Social Democratic Party who threatened disempowering his beloved Kaiser and instituting a programme of progressive change. Rather than face the prospect of being swept aside, these ultra conservatives launched the world's first national social healthcare, pension and employment insurance. They did it not for love of the people but for love of their position. They won their political battle and won the democratic support of their people. The people were delighted with their newly gained benefits until the increased tax bills arrived and the 'small print' of the new insurances became clear.

Ultimately, the German people had been 'thrown a bone'; nothing of any real significance had changed. The Kaiser skimmed the new insurance revenues to improve the military and it became a profit centre for his favoured corporations that administered the programme.

Although this important change improved the lot of the 19th Century German worker it left the feudal structure of society entirely untouched.

The revolutions of France and Russia etc served only to exchange the existing social elite for another. Freeing slaves or enfranchising women were massively needed and merely rectified a serious humanitarian crime but in no way was the ancient social structure, beloved by the Egyptians, affected in any meaningful manner. In no way did these changes effect a true and fair distribution of the Earth's resources. These changes had the affect of providing a temporary distraction from the true transformation that is needed today. Today, we set up protest groups or lobby government in order to make change in areas that do not eliminate the cause of our troubles. When a concession is achieved we celebrate, thinking that everything will magically transform and that our problems are solved, only to find we have so many more problems to deal with.

We are similar to the bull in the ring that keeps on charging at the red cloth, rather than the holder of the cloth. The red cloth may get marked or suffer some damage but the person in control behind the cloth is free to kill another day, after the bull has wasted his huge energies chasing shadows.

Until now, the change we have seen has not affected the ability of those holding money to control and manipulate those without this fantasy item. Now that must change; the bull must recognise the real target of his problems – money.

There is a recognisable historical process to important societal change, which we can identify and use. The process of change is essentially as follows:[89]

1. Identification of a problem by an individual or individuals.
2. An intellectual argument that attracts the educated and influential classes and a message that working people find attractive.
3. The adoption of the cause by a charismatic leader who creates a plan and organises resources.
4. Funding for the idea (usually from the moneyed classes although Barack Obama has shown that fund raising from grass roots can be spectacularly effective).
5. A growing membership that moves beyond the initial special interest group that forces the establishment to accept change simply because of the sheer number of people that demand it. This is sometimes known as critical mass.

The above process for change is entirely repeatable once adjusted for our times and if we choose, we can start the process now.

Our proposal is different in that we are not replacing one pyramidal social structure with another one. The change I'm proposing is a flat power structure with human services organised and distributed by people with no other agenda, who are genuinely public servants. No one is elected to superior power and status and there is no servitude to another person.

Human society has seen so many small changes; we are only using the existing momentum to transform; this idea does not buck the trend. We have seen the decriminalisation of homosexuality and its increasing official/legal acceptance by secular society. We have seen the increasing marginalisation of racism and sexism and secular society is trying to become more tolerant of human difference.

It was only a few hundred years ago we burned eccentric women as witches, or drilled holes in peoples heads to let out the evil spirits. We used not to allow women and black people to vote or own property and we had laws requiring a man to walk in front of a car waving a red flag. The point is that society is constantly making tiny steps towards solving its problems – it's now time to make a giant leap in our progress and deal with the cause of our problems.

Having seen that change is constant, if we band together using effective peaceful methods we can make our governments listen to us and submit to our combined will, we just need a plan.

14

What We Must Change in Ourselves

You must be the change you want to see in the world
Mahatma Gandhi

The first and most important thing we as a group of individuals can do is recognise there is a problem and not just ignore what is happening around us in our name. There is a saying in India that exemplifies our collective problem, *the tears of a stranger is only water.* Society can only change when the individuals that comprise it change themselves.

The Blind Eye

The forces of the status quo depend on our apathy, indifference, our busy-ness and our concern for personal issues closer to home. They depend on us not caring that our neighbour has to accept something that we would not accept for ourselves and our neighbour not caring that we are suffering when they are not.

The following poem was written by Martin Niemöller (1892–1984) to describe the impact of apathy during the troubled years of 20th century Germany:

When the Nazis came for the communists,
I remained silent;
I was not a communist.
When they locked up the social democrats,
I remained silent;
I was not a social democrat.
When they came for the trade unionists,
I did not speak out;

I was not a trade unionist.
When they came for the Jews,
I remained silent;
I was not a Jew.
When they came for me,
There was no one left to speak out.

Our tendency to ignore problems experienced by our neighbours makes it simple for a tiny social elite to divide us, conquer us and abuse us one group at a time. So many malicious leaders have used this weakness in our collective character.

We need to recognise that we are part of an extended family. It is said that in the West, we are all separated by only six or seven friends, relatives or colleagues.[90] This is why genealogists are able to prove family links between the most improbable of people.[91]

When we recognise the fact, that as humans we are all related, that we all contribute to the sum of each others lives, that we all share this little planet, our problems start to diminish because there is less reason to fear other people. We are in life together so let's make heaven here for everyone.

When we learn to stand up for other people, the social elite's grip on power loosens. Our current habit of looking the other way gives an oppressor a free hand to eventually abuse us, not just the people we did not care about. It is the chief device for dividing and conquering and when we realise that the tears of a stranger are as genuine and heartfelt as our own – that is the day that humankind will free itself.

This current human weakness, known as 'Compassion Fatigue' allows us to switch off our interest when other people are suffering.[92] History is replete with examples of the isolation and scape-goating of sub-groups within society. The media and religion came together to support the holocaust in Hitler's Germany and only a few brave people took action to oppose this obviously inhuman behaviour.[93]

People are prepared to accept this kind of treatment for others particularly when financial conditions are difficult or if they have been conditioned to hatred for another group. Some of us have somehow been convinced or we convince ourselves that scapegoats are responsible for our lack of prosperity and that our personal welfare will somehow improve if only we could stop the scapegoats taking our jobs, praying differently, being differently orientated, coming to our country, speaking differently, etc. We convince ourselves that they are somehow responsible for the problems we represent them with, rather than recognise our common humanity and common problems we all share.

The German horror was just another episode in a long chain of terrible events which will continue to happen whilst we live under the tyranny of money. Before the Nazis we had the Inquisitions[94] and since then we have had Kosovo, the terrible ethnic crimes in Liberia, Zimbabwe, Ireland, Tibet, East Timor, problems in Gaza, Iraq and others. This indicates that whilst we put ourselves in the hands of profit driven leaders absolutely nothing will change and these awful crimes against humanity are bound to happen again and again, until we remove the motivation and their opportunity.

We must no longer put ourselves in the hands of profit driven leaders. It is inevitable that eventually we or our descendants will suffer.

Personal Responsibility

There is an additional challenge in our nature that we need to be aware of because the social elite certainly is. We must take action to correct it and teach our children to put it aside. This is our conditioned deference to authority.

The Milgram Experiment of July 1961 found that people were inclined to follow orders from authority figures even if it conflicted with their personal conscience.[95]

Stanley Milgram and numerous follow up experiments found that the majority of us are prepared to murder and harm another human if someone in authority tells us to and if we are able to convince or fool ourselves that we are somehow not responsible for our own actions. Naturally our leaders design working environments to take advantage of this current human weakness. The expression 'I was simply following orders' is, for many, acceptable reason for some of the truly horrific episodes in history.

In 1919 in the Indian city of Amritsar, British soldiers opened fire on a peaceful gathering of civilian men, women and children, killing more than 1,000 and wounding 2,000. The soldiers committed this massacre because their commanding officer told them to.[96] In 1962 in Novocherkassk, Russia, authorities opened fire and killed 87 and injured another 87 hungry food rioters.[97] There is Sharpeville, South Africa;[98] Kent State University, Ohio, USA[99] and there's too many more to catalogue.

This tendency to follow orders regardless of the individual's personal conscience is not restricted to war situations where it could be argued that passions are inflamed. We have examples such as the Tuskegee Study,[100] the German medical experiments on Jews and many more, which indicate that people will calmly and professionally torture, inflict pain upon and humiliate another human being because they are doing what they have been instructed to for the money they will receive.

These terrible events are conducted by apparently normal people with families, friends, hopes, ambitions and dreams. These executioners and torturers also had bills to pay and were 'simply following orders'. They feared for their jobs and were probably thinking that if they were not obedient, someone else would take their means of earning a living.

If these people had simply taken responsibility for themselves, recognized their common humanity, put aside their fear of unemployment and treated their fellow human with the respect they would want for themselves, these things would not happen – no atrocity would ever happen.

Whilst we continue not to think for ourselves and refuse responsibility for our actions, we will continue to live in a world that crushes us and maybe one day we may find ourselves facing a really lovely person 'simply following orders' for the money.

Dr Martin Luther King Jr reminds us that 'everything Hitler did in Germany was legal,' but it was not ethical and not enough people stood up to him. If his followers had simply said, 'No, do it yourself', the history of the world would be so different.

The cure for this potentially awful human weakness is to think for yourself and take responsibility for yourself. Remember to teach your children not to look for excuses, think independently and be brave enough to do the right thing, even if someone is pressuring them not to. This one simple thing would address so many of the world's evils and remove so much negatively used power from those with authority over us.

For the benefit of all mankind we must find our brave human spirit. Many of us remember the iconic image of the student blocking the progress of the tank in Tiananmen Square (June. 1989). If more of us had the courage of that person, the world would be such a different place. However, we are capable of collectively finding our courage and standing up to that machine at any time – it really is our choice.

Remember, it's not just for ourselves, it's for our children and grand-children. We can truly give them a great inheritance – a clean world free from suffering.

15

Questions to Ask Yourself

The issues are much too important for the Chilean voters to be left to decide for themselves.

Henry Kissenger

Before you reject or accept the content of this book there is so much you need to reflect upon. There is so much we can do, but you need to make your own mind up before joining the movement for change.

We can make change but need to be committed and determined before facing this challenge. Your understanding of the problems we face will enhance your commitment to genuine change. Please, therefore, take the time to consider the following currently irresolvable scenarios and questions:

- Cod, haddock and other fish stocks around the northern coasts of Europe are now in severe danger of over-fishing. Fisherman from France, Spain, Portugal, Ireland and others are competing to maximise their catch. Maximising catches encourages the use of equipment that ensnares young fish and virtually everything that gets in the way.

  As a result the European Fisheries Agencies are trying to protect stocks with a protection zone off the Western coasts of the United Kingdom. The fishermen are opposed because they often have non-transferable skills and may not be able to relocate to unfamiliar waters, where the competition will be even fiercer and relocation has costs.

  The Agencies have responded by suggesting that fishing equipment that did not scour the sea clean be used.

The fishermen are objecting because the question is now: who will pay for this new equipment and compensate their reduced income? Who will pay to support unemployed sea workers now and when there are no fish?

Our enslavement to money stops the fishermen and us from doing the things the planet needs. It is not the fault of the fishermen; they are providing for their families, but the planet is forced to pay. It is the failing logic of money that these fish and so many other animals and plants will pay for our short-term needs with extinction.

Even when there are a few cod left and laws are passed to protect them, there will be poachers seeking personal advantage. Money gives the fishermen incentives to do the wrong thing and money gives rich individuals the power to order and pay for the wrong thing.

The same principal applies to all the endangered species that people are hunting and mutilating into extinction.

- What do Henry Kissengers' words (above) tell us about the quality of our leadership and our status in our current democracy? How can our representative refer to *military men* as being *dumb, stupid animals to be used as pawns for foreign policy* if we were anything other than resources to be used and discarded.
- Do we really vote for constant warfare?
- We are told (in the West) that we live in a free and egalitarian society; a democracy that hears our voice and reacts to it. But do we not only have the liberty of our wallet?
- When there is protest from a population, why is it that people only end up being arrested and not listened to?
- Is there a way of registering protest that is effective?
- What kind of democracy do we live in when a leading French politician said 'Public opinion will be led to adopt, without knowing it, the proposals that we dare not present

to them directly ... All the earlier proposals will be in the new text, but will be hidden and disguised in some way'.[101]Why was there no uproar?

- Do we the people direct our own affairs?
- Why is there so much apathy about the political process?
- Have you ever compromised your freedoms or conscience to gain money?
- Do you and your children get access to the best educational and medical resources available; or can you not afford that?
- Why is it that Magic Johnson (a wealthy sports personality) has his HIV managed for so long but it continues to wipe out a generation of other poorer people?
- Would you submit to your daily working routine if you didn't need the cash?
- Will a machine or robot one day take your job? What will you do if that happens?
- How do you benefit when our government leads us into another war?
- How do you feel knowing that civilians in other countries are dying in your name? And that your nationality means you need additional security when you travel or has you treated with suspicion?
- Why is it that governments across the world are finding it necessary to remove our freedoms and spy on us when casualties from terrorism causes less deaths than those caused by avoidable health conditions or car and work accidents?
- Have you ever done anything you are embarrassed about because of money?
- When you hear reports of trouble in other countries, how do you react? Would you be happy with your reaction if the boot was on the other foot?
- With the resources available to government, why hasn't

the drugs trade been halted at source? Who benefits?

- How is it that a chief executive of a failing bank (an institution which manages a totally imaginary commodity) can pay himself $500,000,000.00 in approximately six years; enough to support nearly 500 fully trained nurses for a 40 year working career?[102/103] Has he done anything wrong in accepting that money?

- Why should confidence about the movement of an imaginary commodity make the difference between keeping and losing your home and struggling to feed yourself?

- Why are there countries so poor that their citizens are malnourished yet guns and ammunition never appears to be in short supply?

- How can a country with starving citizens find money to support space exploration or advanced military projects?[104]

- Why should the British Ministry of Defence help design and license toys that portray/encourage war play and killing in children? What does this say about our government's commitment to peace and their plans for our descendents? Is there anything offensive in the fact that royalties from our children's spend is intended to provide funds for future military operations?

- Why do we hunt animals to extinction rather than protect them?

- Why is there a war on terror, rather than a war on sickness, poverty, hunger and homelessness?

- Why do we systematically destroy our natural habitats whilst wilfully disputing the urgency?

- Doesn't everything wrong in the world make perfect sense under the failing logic of money?

But, most importantly...

- Don't we and our children deserve better?

16

The Action We Must Take

Change will not come if we wait for some other person or some other time. We are the ones we've been waiting for. We are the change that we seek.

Barack Obama

Having identified that the most important thing we can do to generate genuine change to our current feudal social structure is to change ourselves and modify our behaviours; there are so many small but accumulatively important things that we can do. It is not necessary to take dangerous or risky actions, neither is it necessary to be involved in any radical activity or street protest (which history has shown do not work alone and is too easily distorted by our media). So many things can be done in the privacy of your home and within the bounds of the law.

At Home
Eliminate Your Debt
It was mentioned earlier that over the centuries, since the Egyptian age, society has changed little. As a means of controlling us, the social elite have only exchanged the whip for debt and unlike those Egyptian slaves; you and I have nowhere to run.

Debt is the principal reason that normal lovely people work at tasks they hate, compromise their nature and subdue their conscience. The tyranny of debt forces people into unhappy relationships makes crime a logical option and truly is the chief instrument of control in the money-based economy.

We are conditioned to accept debt and actively seek it out.

Most Western countries educate our children but leave them with large student debts to start their working lives with and minimal education about personal money management. Our children are financially behind even before they earn their first penny (assuming they can find employment) and once they are employed they find themselves paying elevated taxation to service the debt of the state, a debt which they did not incur and arguably, do not benefit from.

Ditching debt gives us more time, more freedom, more control over what we need to do for money and more opportunity to make decisions that more closely represent our humanity.

An example of how we have been encouraged to spend unnecessarily is the commercialisation of religious holidays. Advertising to excite our children starts months before any actual date and we are encouraged to compete with each other over how much we spend. If we don't indulge in an orgy of gift buying we are somehow made to feel that we are depriving our children and are therefore bad or inadequate parents in some way. The advertising and product promotion industry takes full advantage of this, using children's 'pester power' to make us override our better judgement regarding how we use our money and the foods and gifts we buy our children.[105] As a result we end up seeking more debt to comply with the pressure we put ourselves under. The simplest action we can take is to prioritise our spending.

Don't get caught up in image building or materialism; think for yourself; do not be bullied by the images the media presents. Buy what you need, enjoy your life but don't put yourself in debt for trinkets; remember how much time you need to labour for it, and the interest too. Is it really worth it?

It's not necessary to have the shirt that the celebrity wears. Firstly, the celebrity can easily afford it and most importantly, that person is often being paid to appear in those clothes so that we rush to the shops and get further in debt, emulating these social icons.

The power of the icon is well known to the advertising industry.[106] Successful Soccer players are given vehicles free to use and be seen in, to encourage us to accept debt and delude ourselves that we have that lifestyle. Mike Tyson once reported that the more successful he became, the less he had to pay for. This happens whilst those that really need free help get nothing.

This is crazy, but this is the logic of money.

Without unnecessary debt, how much more quality time would you have if you could translate the money you save into free time or genuine security? Does owning extravagant clothing or a car you can't really afford going to make you happy? If you are going to these troubles to attract someone; will you attract the right person?

Grow Your Own Food and/or Support Your Local Farmer or Food Producer

This way you can ensure the quality of the food you eat and encourage the choice that a financial system inevitably stifles. It is the logic of money that the small supplier will lose out to the giant corporation over time,[107] but we have the power to change that by simply not spending our money there.

Make A Community of Your Neighbours

If you reduce that gap that people have, you'll find friendships, opportunities to help others and be helped. You'll find it is good practice for the world that is coming and good practice for learning to accept and appreciate those little differences between us that highlight just how similar we really are. Develop this further with cooperative endeavours where possible.

Use Your Money Ethically

Support banks and institutions that have nothing to do with war and do not deal with defence contractors. Do not support companies that handle the proceeds of slavery or any other questionable activity. Move your bank account and credit cards if necessary with a letter of explanation, send a signal to those institutions that we are not prepared to accept that kind of activity.

This is such a powerful tool; if we were to remove our savings from a bank or institution that supported the evils of this world, we would bring that organisation to heel overnight and their questionable customers would find themselves being treated as the social pariah they should be. We could force the arms-makers and dealers, the slavers, the illegal animal dealers out of the financial system, just by highlighting and shaming the 'respectable' companies that turn a blind eye, profit from these activities and provide cover, support and services to these people.

Use Your Money Aggressively

Recent financial events have shown that the actions of a tiny number of banking executives can create a huge crisis that requires unprecedented intervention from the tax payer to stop the entire financial system failing. It is possible for a population to re-create this event at any time they chose, collapse the system and implement Earth Economics.

Any demand for deposits to be repaid that exceeds the capital reserve ratio requirement effectively halts the system. Therefore, bank withdrawals that amount to around 20 per cent of the capital base would necessitate government intervention or spell disaster for that individual institution.

Recently in the Netherlands, customers collapsed a bank they were not happy with (DSB Bank) after allegedly misleading its clients. The campaign against DSB Bank was started by one individual and the bank closed within a matter of months. Once the desire for change builds to a critical mass of approximately 20 per cent of the funds held, those in the movement for change can enact a peaceful economic revolution at any time of their choosing.

It is not just those holding money that have the power to end the system, those with debts and expenditures probably have even more power to stop it.

Although I cannot advocate a refusal to pay debts in a coordinated manner, it is likely system failure will occur when the coordinated debt default level was approximately 25 per cent of debt owed. Coordinated refusal to pay taxes would render central government unable to support the failing institutions and helpless to pay the police forces to physically suppress the movement for change. But even if government printed money to pay the police force, a sizeable portion of the population could not be arrested if the action they took was from their home and involved legally transferring funds.

Again, I must repeat that I cannot advocate wilful refusal to pay debts, but another effective method would be to insist on settling debts in cash. The banking system would be unable to cope with the demand for cash, yet there would be no civil disobedience for the government to react negatively to.

Work for Ethical Employers.

If you work for the armed services, defence contractors, vivisectionists, a firm that benefits from treating people in a way that you would not want for yourself and your family – please leave and find another job (remember the level of respect Henry Kissenger has for you).

These things cannot continue without your support and labour. Please find your courage, your heart and your conscience. If you leave, it would all stop overnight and everyone on this planet would hail you as the brave hero you truly are. Very few people actually want to pursue a career in the occupations that we find distasteful, but our need for money causes some of us to override our conscience and accept the task.

Employees of these distasteful organisations should not be bullied or offered stress by the rest of us. These people are only trying to address their human needs in the best way they know. We need to let them know, they are more talented than to compromise themselves. As the momentum for change gathers pace, they will leave those tasks and there will be no one willing to replace them.

Buy Dependency-Reducing Technology

In your home fit renewable energy systems that make sense. Maybe wind turbine or solar technologies or when you need to replace appliances, choose machines with the highest efficiency ratings and the longest replacement cycles. Reducing the running costs of your house allows you that commensurate level of financial freedom.

Think About Your Prejudices

Many of us have conditioned responses towards different cultures, religions, races or lifestyles and maybe this is the time to examine why we have less favourable feelings towards some of the people we meet or see on television.

This is also a key change we need to make. Our attitudes and fears about people are often imposed upon us by the media, our religions, our upbringing or by people who had influence over us. Babies are not born with prejudices or hatred; they are learned from their childhood environment. We need to ask ourselves, who benefits from the prejudices we hold and to honestly examine ourselves to see if anything we have experienced in our own lives gives us genuine reason to support the divisions in humanity. If there are prejudices, ask yourself who does this benefit? Does this really help me and does this really help the world? Do these prejudices stop me appreciating that people from different races, cultures and places are still people, with families, hopes, dreams and fears?

Please realise it is the artificial prejudices that we hold that make it easier for us to deny the genuine human dignity of another person whilst 'following orders' for the money, seeking unfair advantage for ourselves or ignoring the suffering of another human. Remember we or our descendents could one day be victim to the prejudices of another – so let's end it.

If you do find yourself a victim of aggression from another group, before using that experience to judge a whole race or culture, using it to support propaganda or confirm your 'belief' that a group of people are inherently evil – ask yourself, did what happen relate in anyway to 'The Failing Logic of Money'? Was that particular individual unable to find the strength to act honourably in the difficult life they live?

I'm not suggesting that you invite that individual for tea or that they were excusable in any way. But we need to ensure that what happened does not smear an entire race, culture or lifestyle, because there are good and bad, weak and strong, honourable and dishonourable individuals in every group. No culture, religion or race holds a monopoly on virtue or vice. So let's design an environment where negative behaviours are simply unnecessary.

Spread the word

Probably the most important thing we can do initially is talk to people so they understand that there really is a better way of life available. The more people talking about the new economy and the unfixable problems of the financial system we are toiling and suffering under, the bigger the momentum for change that we build. There will come a point, if we work towards it, that our numbers quite naturally overwhelm the status quo and the tiny social elite cannot stand against a determined and purposeful populous.

The above suggestions are intended to reduce our dependence on the current system and its attitudes, to encourage independent thought, highlight our collective strength, demonstrate how fragile our current system is and allow us to disengage from the 'rat-race' and reduce the control that others have over us.

These suggestions will give us a little more time with our loved ones and help us see through the constant distracting and contradictory messages from the media. Being less dependent on the system gives us the luxury of examining it dispassionately and without fear for the repercussions of criticising it or challenging it. These suggestions will bring us closer to our ultimate goal of change and someone wise once said 'the longest journey starts with a single step'.

It may be our children finish the journey, but it could be as soon as we demand it.

Once we have adjusted our lives, recognising the common humanity of all people and are making decisions for ourselves and accepting responsibility for our thoughts, words and actions, there is more we can do.

Defend The Internet

News management is essential for the authorities to follow their agendas without interference from us. If we had known that Iraq was essentially harmless to other countries, would we have sent our sons and daughters to die there? Would we have accepted increases in our taxation to pay for it and provided arms manufacturers, oil corporations, building contractors and private security firms with years of excess profit?

No. The general public is not interested in invading countries where people are trying to live their lives and it gives us absolutely no benefit to do so and no pleasure to see an admittedly unpleasant leader[108] hurriedly hanged.

Scott Ritter (a former UN Weapons Inspector) had been speaking out constantly in the build-up to the invasion, saying that there were no weapons of mass destruction and no justification for an assault. His voice was not heard on mainstream television and radio. Only those that had the time to think for themselves found Scott Ritter on the internet.

Why wasn't Scott Ritter heard? He explains it himself.

His message was not allowed to air because his supervisors were not looking for the truth, but justification for an action already planned. He was willing to talk about it but few in the established media would pursue it. Why?

The answer is plain in a world where the wealthiest one per cent of people own 40 per cent of everything in the entire world. This figure comes from the World Institute for Development, Economics Research Department of the United Nations in 2000. It is simple to see why an unnecessary but profitable war may be encouraged – it is the logic of money. Imagine if you owned an arms factory and business was a little quiet but you had huge influence. It would be tempting to look for business opportunities. Who would blame you because it makes good financial sense?

When you hear of another shocking event, ask yourself, who benefits?

Scott Ritter tried to warn us the only way he could, but we did not hear him. But there are things we can do to ensure that we don't allow this to happen again. Governments are already examining ways of controlling the internet. In totalitarian nations, like China, it is a simple matter of editing the sites and content available to their citizens; even Google succumbed to Chinese government pressure by censoring the searches allowed inside China.[109] China itself has developed a national intranet to exclude any critical information from external sources.[110] This tactic is obviously working because the typical China citizen is unaware of the issues in Tibet and the state closely monitors the media to ensure their citizens remained unaware.[111]

The internet is, therefore, a key way for us as individuals to maintain an understanding of what really is happening around us. We need to establish a website that gives news unfiltered by vested interests or the needs of the social elite.

In Western nations governments are seeking control of the web by more subtle means. In the United Kingdom, government announced plans to trace every website we visit and trace and file every email we send, under its anti-terrorism measures even photographs we look at on social networking websites are logged and recorded by western governments. The government also assumes the power to close down any website it chooses under anti-terror measures and is now seeking to regulate the content of websites by rating every Britain-based site[112] (no doubt a precursor to a new tax).

You may feel that our government would not abuse that authority and the power is needed to protect us but this is proving not to be the case.

The internet is under threat from yet another source. In America, Comcast AT&T, Horizon and other corporations that lay the cables that connect people and business to the web has won the legal right to charge differential rates to those using their cables. This ruling compromises net neutrality and allows the owners of these corporations to charge huge fees to those baring a message they do not like and conversely subsidise those they consider useful.

Net neutrality needs to be protected to allow normal people and the dissenting voice to be heard in the way Scott Ritter never was. We need to protect the last media that is not currently owned and controlled by big business, because if we don't act it soon will be.

Protect Our Civil Liberties

In England, Wales and Northern Ireland local government was given the authority to observe and follow individuals suspected of terrorist connections (under the Civil Contingencies Act 2004, which was rushed through Parliament) and those who may be considered dangerous or involved in the commissioning of serious crime.

This legislation was quickly used by a local authority to ensure that a little girl attended the right school because they thought that the family were abusing the catchments area regulations.

Around 50 per cent of local authorities used the same legislation to observe the way local tax payers used the municipal rubbish collection service.[113] The abuse of available legislation extends to British National Government. A recent example is the use of anti-terror laws to freeze the UK based assets of Icelandic Governmental and private institutions when there is clearly no violent criminal activity in their financial collapse.[114] A similar pattern is being played out in the US with the Patriot Act, where the FBI has been reprimanded for using this act to improperly and, in some cases, illegally, secretly obtain personal information about their own citizens.[115]

The Established Media

Manuel Valenzuela said of the media, *"…he who controls television controls the masses and he who controls the masses controls the nation."*

The importance of who owns and influences the media cannot be overestimated. We have heard it said that if something is repeated often enough, we will eventually believe it even if it doesn't make total sense. Repeating a message 'ad nausium' has the effect of switching off our critical abilities, it was a tactic much used by Hitler to support the slaughter of some of his own people.

Valenzuela went on to say:

"The ruling elite can, through clandestine programming and seemingly innocuous entertainment, influence the way millions of minds think, invariably transforming free thought into shackled reasoning. Over decades of methodical moulding and development, beginning at the earliest age of a human being, those who control

television oftentimes succeed in altering and indeed controlling the opinions, beliefs and thoughts of a person. Thus, the goals and views of the elite are transmuted onto those who stand not to benefit by the beliefs they now possess and the thoughts they have been brainwashed to accept."

The above message is not generated from the viewpoint of a paranoid conspiracist; it is a matter of straightforward logic.

The owners of the media receive funds from advertisers, who in turn receive their funds from us. Therefore, it is commonsense that the media encourages us to consume, to be content with the status quo, not interfere with the plans of our leaders (political and commercial), to not recognise that there is an alternate way of life and basically not to see our power and to accept our lot; to make myself absolutely clear – to lie still while we are milked.

It is essential that we maintain our mental and emotional independence and not be swayed by the messages and images that bombard us.

When the momentum for change to a Earth-based economy starts, you can bet that the established media will howl shrill and dire warnings of doom for us all. It will devote its energies to debunking, derailing, spoiling and sabotage. This will be the social elite trying to defend its entrenched position of privilege. The importance of protecting the integrity of the internet becomes stark, because unbiased reporting is likely to be in even shorter short supply. There are absolutely no circumstances in which we should accept the compromising of our access to or content of the web.

Outside the Home

Having discovered our resolve to see this endeavour through, there are a number of practical things we can do within the limits of our current system. Adding organisation and fundraising to numbers of supporters, we can use the institutions of society to effect change.

Take Back Control of our Political Representatives

Believe it or not, taking control of our society's direction is easy if we have a people with a resolute desire for change. The place to start is with our incumbent politicians. Like everyone else, these people are concerned primarily with their personal standard of living and therefore do and say what is necessary to get elected to office.

Political office gives them numerous opportunities for personal enrichment, which can encourage our representatives to be distracted from their true role of meeting our human needs. They currently measure their success in campaign funds donated by corporations, directorships held whilst in office, income generated by influencing government policy and income to come when they leave office – all whilst trying to garner our votes and give us the impression of a conscientious office bearer.

This can be simply dealt with by only supporting politicians that sign an affidavit where they agree not to accept monies from any other source than their political office. They should also agree to make it a matter of public report if a member of their family accepts a position that could influence our representative. For example, it should not be permissible for the relative of an office bearer to work for lobbyists or any business that can benefit from contacts within government. Naturally, the issue of where they work after leaving office needs to be carefully considered too.

Basically, we should support only the representatives that legally guarantee to have no other financial interest than meeting the needs of those that elect them. This would make them genuinely accountable.

This principal should extend to having them legally guarantee not to make decisions that affect peace, personal freedoms, the environment or the quality of our essential services without a referendum, so we can guide our representatives through the issues of importance to us.

An affidavit would focus their attention on satisfying our needs and at a stroke improve the quality of our politicians whilst ensuring that money interests do not have undue or disproportionate influence over the democratic decision making process. The current situation where deals can be made in smoke filled rooms that start wars or damages our quality of life becomes much less likely.

We should further manage our representatives by making our directives very clear.

We currently allow them to make vague promises; we select them as if they are beauty contestants and then cannot reprove them once they are in office. This needs to change.

Clearly defined targets give them no opportunity to charm, mislead or be vague with us and we would have true transparency to what is essentially a resource administration role with us as beneficiaries. This system would allow us to immediately identify an able administrator and support them or quickly discard an ineffective office holder.

Once our politicians have been managed, we can democratically direct them to implement Earth Economics.

Controlling the Integrity of our News Providers

The power, impact and the misdirected priorities of the media has already been discussed. It is important that supporters of the new world have access to unfiltered news and news that doesn't represent the interests of the social elite. We need to be told which corporations profit from misery, why some people starve among abundance, what our leaders are really doing and the truly pressing issues that our current media has no interest in.

The swiftest way of re-establishing media integrity is to insist that all potential conflicts of interest are made clear to the news consumers or that the agency is disqualified from commenting on that particular issue. For example, if a news outlet is owned by an arms manufacturer it should not be able to broadcast/publish on matters that its parent company can profit from or at least the link should be prominently declared.

We should create an environment where there is no incentive or cause to be anything other than perfectly honest with us.

If our representatives are unable to enact that change, then we create our own trusted agency and support that, basically bypassing the old institutions. Our own independent news agency would also serve as a focal point to our emerging community, promoting our aims and bringing attention to solutions and challenges as we progress to real change.

Our Own Transitional Bank

Having established that there may be banking institutions we should avoid. We can actually be more positive and establish our own bank or build a relationship with an existing banking organisation.

We can use the fractional reserve system to benefit our clients, acquire suppressed patents or support inventions that benefit people but cannot attract assistance from short-term thinkers. This is an opportunity for us to see real progress in making dependency-reducing technologies accessible to the public at reasonable prices.

As our bank grows, it will become a force that cannot be ignored. If we support it, its strength would be assured. Instead of paying dividends to stock or share holders, our bank can support projects that further our aims. With the support of a powerful bank we could acquire land and build a self-sufficient community based upon our principals and show the world what we can achieve.

It can work from the 'inside' to improve our world. It would be well-placed to track the movements of money identifying the beneficiaries, the corrupt and the inhumane. A bank would give us access to the tools and privileges that have been used against us for centuries. Our own bank, strong with our support, would present us with a truly formidable weapon against the tyranny of money – 'fighting fire with fire'. With an international reach, it would soon be able to conduct an audit of the key world resources as part of its business activities.

The international banking system currently has knowledge of the activities of virtually every person, small business and corporation in the world. To have any dealings with the banking system, a person must identify himself and provide extensive personal and occupational information. The banks also know how you spend your money, where you like to spend it and track your movements through the payments you make with your credit and debit cards. The system can track any exchange of goods for money and has an information gathering reach that is actually quite shocking.

With the information that a bank has access to, it will be able to identify the geographic placement, the availability and the logistical requirements of all the resources that we need to support human life and the luxuries that we (in the prosperous nations) have become accustomed to.

With this information and the financial might of our support, our bank can ease the transition from a money society to the new system. Once the task is achieved, the bank can either close down or transition into the coordination administration committee that the new society will need.

Our Own Charitable Institution

As we trade (with each other nationally and internationally), our financial strength will become significant, which we can use to make change. We can use our own charity to develop and improve the technologies the new world order will need and implement them in real world situations, bringing relief to those currently suffering.

The First Step

It would require one well resourced country to start the change we want to cause the other money-based economies to join our fold. During this transitional period it maybe necessary to maintain some forms of national deterrent capability purely to stop other countries attempting to aggressively swart progress. But once the change is complete the tools of war will be totally unnecessary.

The banking arm will be able to identify which countries are capable of creating a successful start to a new economy, having identified all the key resources, assets, infrastructure and logistics that will be needed and it can preside over an orderly transition. Naturally, there will be pains but with our goodwill, organisation and resolve we will be able to withstand, succeed and prosper.

17

Conclusion to Book Three

Together We Can Make it Happen

What difference does it make to the dead, the orphans and homeless, whether the mad destruction is wrought under the name of totalitarianism or the holy name of liberty or democracy?

Mahatma Gandhi

This book has no doubt challenged preconceptions and hopefully helped you recognise your powerful status but you are probably still thinking that there is no way that society can change so radically.

We have already discussed the ingredients of change but it is human nature not to attempt something that we feel may be impossible, or something that we feel has never been achieved before. The fear of something new has contributed to our acceptance of the world's problems and our personal servitude to money.

We have discussed the plan we can follow for us to retake control of our lives and our humanity. We know we have the necessary technology to make the transition and fulfil the intent of the American Indian, and I am optimistic that humankind is approaching the emotional maturity needed to make our endeavour successful. We must never forget that the way we live now is just a moment in the board sweep in the history of humankind (we used to live in caves). Much has passed before us, and there is so much more change to come. Change is inevitable and it's welcome, just look how far we have come in your lifetime, in your grandparents lifetime and since our caveman ancestors.

My biggest fear for this necessary change is that people will remain content to live with their invisible chains, content to be told what to think, what to do and continue to work to pay taxes which are then used to create misery in the lives of others. I fear that people will think that change cannot be achieved.

There are small pockets of this new way of life if you look for it: in our homes and with our close friends and families we happily give or exchange resources without seeking undue advantage or punitive reward. With our families we do not hoard and compete unfairly. We know how we should be living because most of us live it everyday with those close to us. We just need to widen our definition of family and remember to never accept or impose upon someone something we would not accept for ourselves.

It is the old adage, 'do unto others', but it is about time that we did more than just pay it lip service or apply it selectively.

If you look carefully you will see small communities that are already living to the principals of the Earth Economics:

There are fundamentalist religious groups in America and elsewhere that live self-sufficiently on their land in virtually cashless communities; these groups have chosen to reject our current modern life. They also tend to reject technology in any form preferring to conduct physical labour themselves.

We are seeking to achieve what these people have but to avail ourselves of every appliance, every labour-saving device, every convenience of science and medicine, and for it to be freely available to all.

Automated ecological factories can run day and night providing us all with the goods we want. Our houses could be made to order and assembled in automated factories then delivered to site, with clean energy sources (such as Photovoltaics) built into the structure. A clean, safe vehicle could be delivered to each of us from an automated factory that freely builds in the options we require and that vehicle being freely replaced when it is obsolete.

Think of our foods grown and reared sustainably. There will be respect for the consumers, the animal life involved and automated systems replacing human labour where-ever possible.

Think of the people that truly want to work in this area doing so with love and care, their workload shared among many. Imagine human services delivered freely by people who genuinely want to help and are happy doing what they love rather than what they must to survive.

Envisage people thinking carefully about family planning because there is no financial advantage or disadvantage in having children; the children we do have being treated the way they should. Think of people with time and freedom to educate themselves and make informed choices.

Imagine no financial stresses for anyone at all, with each member of humanity being free to challenge him or her self in any direction they chose and contribute to society in anyway they can.

When all of the above happens, each and every one of us will live to a standard that kings as little as 100 years ago would envy.

This is our birthright. We really can build heaven right here, right now.

We can put aside our wasteful, adversarial and primitive way of distributing resources and abolish scarcity.

We can respect the humanity of every person, abolish servitude, oppression, fear and the reason for crime.

We can foster independence, compassion, peace, cooperation, tolerance and love for every human alive and provide our children with a world that is wonderful for all.

Now, imagine doing something about it.

Post Script

The new world order will require its citizens to take a new, active, involved approach to how we generate, manage and distribute our resources; balancing responsibility with rights, and wants with what the planet and technology can sustainably provide us.

To ensure that no new tyrannies can develop it would be essential that the population keep ever vigilant and one way to achieve this is a Constitution or Contract with society that a young adult could be asked to sign.

During my research and writing of this book I have often envisaged how life would be after the change to Earth Economics and I submit this Agreement with society and our planet for your debate.

I hope this speculative document helps you to visualise the society that is coming when the dust settles after the inevitable collapse of our current money based system.

A Citizen's Agreement

Congratulations on reaching the age of legal majority (19) and completing your compulsory education.

This is a day to celebrate because you have the opportunity to become a valued citizen; contributing and benefiting, with responsibilities and rights within our community.

This Agreement is a Code of Conduct with two Chapters; the first with the planet upon which we all depend, and secondly, with the inhabitants of the planet.

The key institution of the community is the Coordination Administration Committee. The role of this organisation is to serve the community and planet by managing resources to ensure that all people have the expected standard of living.

The members of the committee are democratically selected from the various regions of the world and each position is devolved to three individuals with a maximum four year term. This arrangement ensures that no individual can seek or exercise authority beyond the remit of the service, or attract personal authority.

The Coordination Committee/Administration's function is to respond to the needs of the community and planet. The community determines its own needs using the democratic process and community debate forums. Committee/Administration members are not permitted to have any influence or representation during the community's process of objective setting.

The committee has no authority over the other institutions affecting human affairs such as the Election organisers, Community Police, Code of Citizens Conduct Body (formally known as the law) or the media. This separation of responsibilities is enshrined. Each institution has a similar process of changing its leading figures; however, each institution changes them in such a way as to prevent the possibility of entrenchment or collusion across the institutions which are there to serve the community.

The Agreements are subject to review should the community demand so with a 75 per cent majority vote and the key service organisations are similarly subject to review.

Chapter One – Preamble to Agreement with the Planet

Our Planet, the environment, animal and plant life sustains and supports every activity and endeavour a human can attempt. It is, therefore, imperative that she is treated with the utmost respect and that human activity has minimal impact on our planet.

It is our overriding principal that the planet is held in trust for future generations; it is not ours to destroy, damage or sequester for the benefit of a few.

To support this aim you agree to never knowingly cause harm or distress to the planet and the environment without authorisation to do so. Authorisation will only take the form of express written permission in pursuance of a duly approved Coordination Committee project directive.

There are absolutely no other circumstances in which ecological harm or cruelty is acceptable.

Your ecological responsibilities extend to it being an offence to allow another individual to harm the planet without bringing the infraction to the attention of the media and the Committee.

Chapter Two – Preamble to Agreement with Society

As a citizen, you are entitled to all the rights and privileges unless you act outside of the Code of Conduct or breach its terms.

Violation of the Code of Conduct will result in a Tribunal of Peers, assessing the extent to which this Agreement has been broken and selecting the appropriate response, ranging from withdrawal of privileges, Community Service or solitary exclusion from society by way of an automated correctional facility.

The responsibilities you are to discharge as a citizen are in outline as follows.

1. To respect the human dignity of all people. To allowing each to practice their religious or other convictions without interference insofar as they do not impact upon your own ability to pursue your religious or other convictions or those of any other.

2. Not to support by silence or apathy those who do not respect the human dignity of others.

3. To respect property (personal, municipal and other) except insofar as there is no conflict with the human needs of yourself and others. Human needs have priority.

4. To accept responsibility for your own actions and to support, protect and care for your children and children of the community.

5. To cooperate with the institutions of the community; however, you are requested to remain vigilant to ensure that these institutions do not exceed their sole remit, which is to respond to and serve the needs of the community, as the community democratically directs

6. To contribute to the community by providing five years Community Service by way of Higher Education or research in your chosen subject. You can nominate your community service in non-academic areas of your choice. This service is not to exceed 30 hours per week and 45 weeks per year.

7. To further contribute to society after the initial five year service has expired, with a commitment of 10 hours per week, 40 weeks per year (more is your choice but brings no further advantages other than personal satisfaction) in the area of your choice.

8. Failure to discharge your responsibilities to the community results in your privileges and rights being restricted, suspended or removed. This is particularly the case if you are judged to have infringed upon the human dignity of another person, or caused unauthorised suffering to animals and/or ecological harm.

9. Any children born to you or fathered by you during your initial Community Service period will not interrupt your responsibilities to the community. You will be required to seek parental support from the co-parent, the extended families, friends, and as a last resort, the community itself (by way of community homes).

10. It is your responsibility to participate in democratic decision making when the committee requires guidance from the community.

Having established your responsibilities it is appropriate to outline the privileges you are entitled to as a member of our community.

1. You are entitled to live without fear of lacking anything essential to sustaining life. Freely provided.

2. You are entitled to pursue your interests, studies, activities, etc, without hindrance insofar as they do not impact upon the human dignity of another person or bring harm to the planet. Your time is your own.

3. The community will provide you with protection against any person/s intent on disrespecting your rights.

4. You are entitled to have your views on civic and committee matters considered within the democratic decision making process.

5. You are entitled to freely use the national and international transportation system and accommodation services provided by the community.

6. After two years of satisfactory community service you will be freely provided with single or couple living accommodation and a personal transport vehicle of your choice should you require it. Until that time you are expected to remain under the guidance of your parents wherever possible.

7. After concluding your initial Community Service, should you wish to begin your own family life, you will be provided with family accommodation and a family vehicle.

8. You and your family are entitled to use all the facilities of the community without obligation. If there are additional facilities that you require the Committee would be willing to arrange it if there is sufficient support from the community and the resources are available.

9. You are entitled to serve on the Committee or within the institutions that serve the community should you be selected to do so by your peers.

By signing the Agreement with the planet and the Agreement to those that inhabit the Planet you are welcome to fully contribute to and benefit from our community. If, however, you feel unable to accept the terms of these agreements you are entitled to live within the parental family home and benefit from the public services available to the parental family. You will not be required to contribute to the Community and will be considered a burden of the state.

You will be subject to the regulations concerning behaviour within the community and will be subject to the sanctions and appropriate disciplines.

You will not be able to participate in the democratic processes nor hold any positions of service to the community.

You will, however, be offered the opportunity to sign the Agreements and become a citizen after a five year hiatus and any time thereafter. However, your Community Service obligations will commence from the date of your signing and your ability to gain community benefits will commence after four years of service instead of two years. Thereafter, your status reverts to that of any citizen.

Appendix:

Proving the Link between Crime & Poverty

Poverty is the Mother of Crime

Marcus Aurelius Antorimus

The issue of a link between poverty and crime has long been academically studied and strongly established. The majority of studies indicate there is a causal link ie, poverty creates crime. However, there is a minority opinion that crime creates poverty. My research has found those that adopt the minority opinion generally tend to be politically right of centre. They argue that crime causes insurance costs to increase, property values to decrease and increased costs of maintaining property appearance and its contents causing poverty. Additionally, they argue that the more financially able people leave the declining area thus reducing the general standard of living for those that remain.

The majority academic view is that poverty forces individuals to commit crime and I would argue, in order to meet their human need. However, poverty is mostly a relative condition which is measured in comparison to their immediate surroundings i.e., in the prosperous west an individual is likely to feel impoverished if they cannot afford a mobile phone, they do not subjectively measure their poverty in absolute terms against an international standard.

For the purposes of this book, it is irrelevant which came first because either cause requires resources to create change.

The following clearly illustrates this point. If crime begets poverty, then the solution is to deploy significant anti-crime resources in the relevant areas, boosting police presence and resources in such a way as to stop the possibility of the community members successfully completing a crime. This would eventually lead to prosperity, although there would be human rights issues.

If however, poverty generates crime, then the solution is to deploy significant anti-poverty initiatives in the relevant areas, boosting benefits, work creation schemes and social services in such a way as to make crime un-necessary. This would directly lead to a more prosperous community.

But both potential solutions need significant investment for a successful outcome. This investment can only come from taxing the more prosperous (thus reducing their standard of living) and creating divisions in society as the prosperous lobby to protect themselves and ignore the needs of the less well off.

Professor Steve Levitt of University of Chicago concluded that a five percent increase in US unemployment rates generate about five percent increase in property crime. A study conducted by Roger Houchin of Glasgow Caledonian University School of Life Sciences showed a link between crime and poverty in 2004/2005. The National Retail Federation 2009 Crime Survey (www.nrt.com) indicated that 67.5 per cent of its members had seen a year on year increase of at least 25 percent in theft and robberies. The Association of Convenience Stores has also recently announced huge increases in shop crime. The University of Leicester found that cheap imported electronic goods have encouraged some burglars to become muggers and robbers to steal iPods and mobile telephones. The British Crime Survey has found that domestic burglaries have increased for the first time in six years at the start of this latest recession.

There is also clearly observable evidence in terms of comparing the crime rates in different nation states. Luxembourg has probably the world's highest income per person and is certainly one of the world's safest places to live. Compare this to The Republic of Congo, Zimbabwe, Bolivia or Mexico.

Either way our representatives in government appear

reluctant to make the needed resources available and because of this, more communities and people become marginalised and caught up in that poverty – crime – poverty cycle.

The link is clear, it really doesn't matter which came first.

References and Notes

1   In the United States, a 2001 UN survey found that 10 per cent of the population held 71 per cent of the wealth and the top 1 per cent control 38 per cent, meanwhile the poorest 40 per cent of people share 1 per cent between them.

2   *Recession will bring a big rise in crime and race hatred says Home Office.* The Times, 1 September 2008. *Recession Draws Amateurs to crime.* The Patriot Ledger, 3 January 2009, *Is Recession behind spike in bank robberies?* CNN News, 31 December 2008.

3   Maslow's accepted theory 'The Hierarchy of Need'.

4   America introduced taxation to pay for the Civil War (1861-1865) and the UK in 1798 as the tax to beat Napoleon (www.hmrc.gov.uk)

5   In the early 1300's King Philip IV of France (known as Philip the Fair) found it necessary to destroy the Knights Templar to avoid the debt he owed them and the power his creditors held over him. *ABC News*, Australia, 26 October 2007.

6   Between 1649 and 1660 in England there were a number of non-conformist groups seeking to reform the social order to be more religious or most often to be more equitable. These groups included Levellers, Barrowists, Familists, Seekers and many more. Europe was also experiencing its own social issues.

7   www.history.org.uk

8   www.antislavery.org

9   *Bloomberg News*, 7 November 2008

10 *The Bank Credit Analysis Handbook: A Guide for Analysts, Bankers and Investors,* Jonathan Golin. Published by John Wiley and Sons 2001.

11 When all currency had to be backed by the equivalent holding of gold.

12 Every banknote has approximately seven times its value held on computerised account ledgers, see note 10.

13 Such as investing in the creative activities of others, trading loan bonds and other financial paper and of course drawing contracts.

14 CJD is just one illness there is concern about being spread through foods consumed. *The Observer*, 3 August 2008.

15 The World Health Organisation estimates that there are one million serious poisonings every year, especially in developing countries from handling the chemicals we will eventually eat.

16 *One Hundred Per Cent Safe? GM Foods In The UK*, Vivian Moses, visiting professor of biotechnology at King's College, London, and Dr Michael Brannan, a biochemist. Both are senior associates of CropGen. CropGen is a body funded by the GM industry.

17 *Regulatory systems for GE crops a failure: the case of MON863*, Greenpeace. March 2007.

18 *Media & Culture Journal, Vol 11* (2008) – *Equal* – John Paull (Blind peer reviewed).

19 rBST was banned in Europe in 1993 and the ban lifted in year 2000. In America, rBST has been used since 1994; in Vermont a law requiring rBST labelling was passed in September 1995. In January 1999, Canada banned rBST because they found a 25 per cent increase in mastitis in cows, an 18 per cent increase in infertility and double the risk of becoming lame. *The Farlex Dictionary & Hutchinsons*.

20 Canadians for Rational Health Policy, indicate that Pfizer, SmithKline Beecham and others own the suppliers of herbal and other alternative medicine providers.

21 www.progressiveu.org identifies Bayer as knowingly releasing tainted drugs into several non-American markets.

22 Felidamide is still being used but administered with caution.

23 www.dorway.com

24 Vance Packard has written extensively on this subject.

25 *The Car That Ran on Water*, The Columbus Dispatch, 8 July 2007

26 *The Trillion Dollar Defence Budget is Already Here*, Robert Higgs. The American Chronica, March 17, 2007.

27 *Who Holds the Wealth of Nations*, Andrew Rozanov. Senior Manager. Official Institutions Group, State Street Global Advisors. In Central Banking, Journal Vol XV, Number 4, May 2005.

28 130,000 people were employed in several secret locations on the Manhattan Project.

29 A recent study indicated that more people knew who Bart Simpson was than could name our Secretary of Defence: the person that literally presides over the deaths of thousands of people.

30 CBS, formally known as Viacom, has links to Westinghouse Electric Systems now Northrop Grumman Electronic Systems.

31 www.fair.org

32 In February 2003, a Florida Court of Appeals unanimously agreed with an assertion by FOX News that there is no rule against distorting or falsifying the news in the United States. www.projectcensored.org

33 The Sun newspaper, 11 April 1992.

34 www.imb.org

35 US Census Bureau 2009 Survey

36 www.namesofthedead.com

37 Medical Bankruptcy in the US 2007, Himmelstein, DE et al.

38 Los Angeles Times, 17 June 2009

39 NBC News 11 – 9 October 2009

40 www.healthreformwatch.com

41 www.cnn.com, 14 June 2006

42 New York Times, 25 March 2009

43   In America alone 2008 saw personal bonuses of US$18.4b to Wall Street executives – CNN 23 October 2008

44   www.thinkprogress.org

45   Metro Newspaper, 12 February 2010

46   Huffington Post, 22 February 2010

47   www.care2.com

48   *From Lynching to Gay-Bashing: The Elusive Connection between Economic Conditions and Hate Crime.* Journal of Personality and Social Psychology, 1998.

49   *London police warn recession will boost crime*, Reuters, 6 January 2009.

50   Rosemary Hopcroft, a University of North Carolina sociologist, advises that rich men have fewer children.

51   www.homelessamerican.com

52   *Down and Out in Europe*, Time Magazine, 10 February 2003.

53   The Guardian Newspaper, 27 January 2010

54   *Gated Communities More Popular*, USA Today, 16 December 2002

55   Elizabeth Mytton, a psychologist, says of celebrities they 'can be quite unhappy people. They can become quite isolated by their fame.' She advises that for many performers, the original spur to fame was an urge to be loved, but they can find that their success, in fact, cuts them off from people.

56   *The Psychological Consequences of Money, Kathleen D. Vohs, Nicole L. Mead, Miranda R. Goode from the University of Minnesota, Florida State University and University of British Colombia, respectively. They found that having money had a negative affect on inter-personal relationships.*

57   According to www.am-online.com, one Toyota factory in France makes 270,000 cars per year, approximately 740 cars per day.

58   The Fall, Steve Taylor

59   www.endpoverty2015.org, www.womenaid.org, the UN

World Food Programme and
www.wm.edu/as/publicpolicy/news/homelessness.php

60   The United Nations already does this on an annual basis
      through its Development Programme.

61   Environmental Management: American Indian Knowledge
      & The Problem of Sustainability – Leaf Hillman & John F
      Salter.

62   *Abundance versus Scarcity Mentality,* Harry Owens, Jr.,
      MD,MIM, CPE, FACPE, St. Charles Medical Centre, Bend,
      Oregon.

63   *Unsold foreign cars pile up at U.S. Port,* 24 November 2008.
      www.thestar.com.

64   In 1994, Staffordshire University Business School published
      the results of a survey indicating that 1 in 2 UK employees
      have been bullied at work during their working life.

65   *More than 5 Million People are working Unpaid Overtime in the
      UK,* Trade Union Congress, 6 January 2009.

66   SHRM – www.Careerajournal.com in conjunction with
      Gallop.

67   www.ukpollingreport.co.uk indicates that only around 50
      per cent of eligible voters do so, apathy being a significant
      cause.

68   *Benefits of higher education for employers and employees,*
      www.hero.ac.uk

69   George W Bush is the only President without published
      books and papers prior to his presidency. He completed
      university with a 'C' grade average and his business career
      started with an oil business in Texas that subsequently
      failed, before he commenced his political career.

70   *British adults 'fear youngsters',* BBC News, 22 October 2006.

71   HM Government Home Office statement: 'The links
      between drug use and crime are clearly established. In fact,
      around three-quarters of crack and heroin users claim they
      commit crime to feed their habit'.

72 Granted by Elizabeth I, December 1600.

73 Professor at University of Wisconsin-Madison. The Politics of Heroin in South East Asia. Harper & Row, 1972.

74 60 Minutes (Investigative Television Show), CBS Channel. Nov 1993

75 *Social Norms as Under Appreciated Sources of Social Control*, R. Cialdini Published in Psychometrika Vol 72, No. 2.

76 *The car that stops you drink-driving*, The Daily Mail, 4 August2007

77 www.wnrf.org: website for the World Network of Religious Futurists.

78 *Field Calibration and Monitoring of Soil-Water Content with Fibre-glass Electrical Resistance Sensors*, Soil Science Society Journal of America, 1993.

79 *Comparative and Absolute Production Efficiency Analysis*, Robert Torrens, 1815 economic theory.

80 *Growth terms of trade and comparative advantage*, Economia Internazionale, 1959. Jagdish Bhagwati.

81 *Khat Commerce In Ethiopia Is Booming*, The United States Mission in Ethiopia (2000)

82 *Farmers of Ethiopia turn to khat as world coffee prices tumble*, (Oxfam) www.globalexchange.org, 8 December 2003.

83 These buyers are Sarah Lee, Kraft, Nestle, Proctor & Gamble.

84 *The 24seven Health Plan*, Christopher Pick N.D. and *Overview of The Implications and Concerns of Agricultural Land Retirement in the San Joaquin Valley, California*, Beatrice A. Olsen and Curtis E. Uptain

85 Source for this comment: www.nutraingredients-usa.com

86 www.teslamotors.com

87 www.o-keating.com

88 For America: www.cdc.gov and for Great Britain: www.statistics.gov.uk

89 *The Anatomy of Revolution*, Crane Brinton. Referenced in The

Structure and Dynamics of Networks. Norman, Barabasi & Watts, Princeton University Press, 2006.

90 *Contacts and Influence: A Study of Social Networks*, Manfred Kochen.

91 For example, Barack Obama is related to Dick Cheney; George Bush is related to Queen Elizabeth II and many more.

92 *Traumatic Stress & The News Audience*. Dart Centre for Journalism and Trauma. June 2008.

93 Homosexuality, immigration, race, gender, religion, status have all been used to ferment disunity.

94 Millions were tortured and murdered for following a different faith and to acquire their wealth.

95 *Obedience to Authority; An Experimental View*, Stanley Milgram. Harper Perennial, 1974.

96 Home Political Deposit, September, 1920, No 23, National Archives of India, New Delhi; Report of Commissioners, Vol I, New Delhi.

97 *A History of the Soviet Union*, Geoffrey Hosking

98 *The Sharpeville Massacre – A watershed in South Africa*, Rt. Reverend Ambrose.

99 *The day the Vietnam War came home*, John Lang. Of Scripps Howard News Service (5 Apr 2000)

100 The Tuskegee Study of Untreated Syphilis in the Negro Male. 'Syphilis Victims in U.S. Study Went Untreated for 40 Years; SYPHILIS VICTIMS GOT NO THERAPY', J Heller.

101 V.Giscard D'Estaing, Le Monde, 14 June 2007, and Sunday Telegraph, 1 July 2007

102 International Herald Tribune, 18 September 2008.

103 www.payscale.com

104 www.isro.org and www.economywatch.com.

105 *Food Advertising, Pester Power, and Its Effects*, International Journal of Advertising, November 2006.

106 Celebrities are used to sell us everything from toothpaste to

fragrances to fashion.

107 *Wal-Mart roll-back hits high street; City analysts are overhauling their retail ratings as Asda unveils another £37m in price cuts,* The Independent on Sunday, 14 October 1999.

108 Allegedly, employed by American CIA.
     Remember: Saddam was our man, New York Times, March 14, 2003.

109 *Google adheres to the Internet censorship policies of China,* BBC News, 31 January 2008.

110 According to the Carnegie Endowment for International Peace.

111 *How Much Do the Chinese Know About Tibet? Chinese Government Censors Clamping Down on News of Protests,* Jo Ling Kent, ABC News, 20 March 2008.

112 *Culture secretary Andy Burnham wants cinema-style age ratings for websites,* The Guardian, 27 December 2008.

113 'More than half of councils are using anti-terror laws to spy on families suspected of "bin crimes", it has emerged'. The Telegraph, 1 November 2008.

114 'Icelandic PM: "terrorist law must not be applied to Iceland."' Icelandic Daily News, 9 October 2008

115 'FBI Violations May Number 3,000, Official Says', The Washington Post, 21 March 2007.

Further Reading

The Fall: The Insanity of the Ego in Human History and the Dawning of a New Era. Steve Taylor – O Books 2005.

Money, transportation, Land and Labour. The People Slaves. The Monopolists Masters. Cary Smith – Dodge City Times 1888.

Confessions of an Economic Hitman. John Perkins – Plume 2005.

The Return of Scarcity: Strategies for an Economic Future. Coombes – Cambridge University Press 1990.

Moneyless Government: Or, Why and Why Not? Henry McCowen – Wetzel Pub Co 1933.

The Best That Money Can't Buy: Beyond Politics, Poverty & War. Jacques Fresco – Global Cybervisions 2002.

Nomads of the Borneo Rainforest: The Borneo Economics, Politics and Ideology of Settling Down. Sellato & Morgan – University of Hawaii Press 1994.

Equity, the Third World and Economic Delusion. Bauer – Harvard university Press 1981.

The Ethics of What We Eat: Why Our Food Choices Matter. Singer & Mason – Rodale 2006.

History of Economic Thought. Kapp – Barnes & Noble 1949.

Poverty, Crime and Punishment. Dee Cook – Child Poverty Action Group 1997.

The Causes of War. Geoffrey Blainey – Free Press 1988.

The Case Against the Fed. Rothbard – Ludwig von Mises Institute 1994.

Wealth, Poverty and Starvation: An International Perspective. George – Prentice Hall 1988.

***Soon to be Published – The Barefoot Revolution. Mullin

www.DuaneMullin.com

B O O K S

O is a symbol of the world, of oneness and unity. In different cultures it also means the "eye," symbolizing knowledge and insight. We aim to publish books that are accessible, constructive and that challenge accepted opinion, both that of academia and the "moral majority."

Our books are available in all good English language bookstores worldwide. If you don't see the book on the shelves ask the bookstore to order it for you, quoting the ISBN number and title. Alternatively you can order online (all major online retail sites carry our titles) or contact the distributor in the relevant country, listed on the copyright page.

See our website www.o-books.net for a full list of over 500 titles, growing by 100 a year.

And tune in to myspiritradio.com for our book review radio show, hosted by June-Elleni Laine, where you can listen to the authors discussing their books.

MySpiritRadio